# THE BOY FROM PLASTIC CITY

# THE BOY FROM PLASTIC CITY

*Reminiscences of a Mill Town Rebel*

by John Tata

FELLOW
PILGRIM
BOOKS

*Dedicated to Helen and Tony*

# ESSAYS

| | |
|---|---|
| The Raft | 1 |
| The Plastic City | 3 |
| My View | 7 |
| Plastic | 9 |
| Injection Molding | 11 |
| Ritual | 13 |
| Trudy and Moe | 17 |
| Concord Rotary | 21 |
| Red Ryder | 23 |
| The Cave | 27 |
| Galaxy 500 | 31 |
| Knockmanagh | 37 |
| Night Games | 41 |
| Katzenjammer Kids | 45 |
| The Phoenix | 47 |
| East Side Loop | 53 |
| Kilroy Was There | 57 |
| Mass | 61 |
| The Divil Ye Know | 65 |
| Old Mill Road Monster | 69 |
| I Was A Teenage Caveman | 73 |
| The Cats | 77 |
| Telstar | 81 |
| Lady of Spain | 85 |
| A Sleeping Prophet | 89 |
| Raison D'être | 93 |
| Aurora | 95 |
| White Sands | 99 |
| Homers | 103 |
| Papermaker | 105 |
| Showdown | 109 |
| Whitney Field | 111 |

| | |
|---|---|
| The Kingdom | 115 |
| Duel of the Titans | 121 |
| A Grenade in the Garden | 125 |
| Season of War | 131 |
| Monorail | 135 |
| Cortege | 139 |
| The '56 | 143 |
| Human Cannonballs | 147 |
| The White Ghost | 153 |
| Junk | 157 |
| Egg Nacht | 163 |
| My Red Room | 167 |
| Nature's Way | 171 |
| White Noise | 177 |
| Egypt | 183 |
| Omerta | 189 |
| Xin Loi | 193 |
| Cat's Eye | 197 |
| Pinnacles | 201 |
| The Box | 205 |
| Centenarian | 207 |
| Doctor Wu | 213 |
| The Patch | 217 |
| Nine One One | 221 |
| The Barn | 229 |
| Fairmount | 233 |
| Flyer Comet | 237 |
| Cholame | 243 |
| Hula Hula | 249 |
| Poor Little Fool | 253 |
| Sun Records | 261 |
| Memphis | 265 |
| Good Night Irene | 269 |
| My Pictures | 275 |

*West Fitchburg, Massachusetts, 1948*

# ACKNOWLEDGEMENTS

**When I took my** first tentative stab at blogging this memoir in 2010—after commenting that some aspects of my childhood had a "...Tom Sawyer/Huck Finn" quality—I posted, "I'm creating this today in order to sort through some memories and jot them down, frankly, before I forget them. Wish me luck." Within minutes I received a comment from **Bohemian Butterfly** who lists her whereabouts as India. "Good luck Huck Finn," she wrote. Knowing that one person had read my post was enough impetus to keep me writing. Since then I've had the honor of thousands of reads all over the world—a fact for which I am most grateful.

My mother's two remaining siblings, **Peg** and **Bob**, provided details from her life and times for which I offer thanks. I'm indebted as well to **Geno Gentile, Dave Bak, Jean Binda, Nunzio Nano, Tom Flynn, Rueben Barrio, Linda Pinder, Louie Luongo** and of course my **Jocelyn** for guidance, encouragement and, best of all, unpaid labor.

# THE BOY FROM PLASTIC CITY

Mildred: "Hey Johnny, what are you rebelling against?"
Johnny: "Whadda you got?"

— From *The Wild One*


Mr. McGuire: "I just want to say one word to you. Just one word."
Benjamin: "Yes, sir."
Mr. McGuire: "Are you listening?"
Benjamin: "Yes, I am."
Mr. McGuire: "Plastics."
Benjamin: "Exactly how do you mean?"

— From *The Graduate*

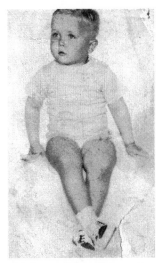

*The Boy from Plastic City*

# FOREWORD

**The essays collected in this book** began as an effort to sort through some memories and jot them down before I forget them. It is the offshoot of my blog of the same name. I thought that blogging stream-of-consciousness-style would allow me to gather my thoughts and stories without getting bogged down with the chronology, and it did, so it is not an autobiography *per se*. Now that they are collected, I could put them into order, but somehow that does not play as well, at least to my mind.

Over the years I have repeated anecdotes from my early days in Leominster, Massachusetts and some people have found amusement in them. Someone once called it a "magical Tom Sawyer/Huckleberry Finn childhood." I would not go that far but some weird/scary/funny and sad things did happen.

In those days (1950s and '60s), in that place (French Hill), it should be said, that when not in school, we left our homes and walked off into our own little lives like those ghostly baseball players who disappear into the corn rows in the film *Field of Dreams* quite on our own. But rather than cornstalks, we disappeared into the lakes, fields, forests and swamps that we haunted.

The events depicted on these pages are an amalgam of memories, imagination, hearsay, artistic license, folklore, embellishment and...*Truth*. I confess to writing the legend if it was more fun than the fact. This is how I remember it and I have endeavored to relate it in an entertaining way—but not at the expense of embarrassing my cast-of-characters. I have striven to be gentle on everyone (but myself). For this reason I have refrained from using last names and in a couple of instances used aliases. Still, if I've offended anyone, I'm sorry. That was not my intent. Neither was it my intent to suggest that group photos implied gang/club membership, affiliation or activity.

Those who ran in the same circles all those years ago might well guess the players, or themselves, from the incidents described. If they do, they should know that they are my ghosts and that I love them.

*John Tata*
*Magnolia, Massachusetts*
*December 29, 2015*

*Boots for Christmas*

# THE RAFT

*Prelude:*

*Where to begin? Since I've evoked (and invoked) Huck Finn, it seems appropriate to start with the story of the raft, which is closer to the beginning of my collection of tales than to the middle of them. It is not the most dramatic or funny of the lot, but I think it captures a certain essence of that time and place and serves to set the stage. With that, let us pole off.*

&

**A kid from my neighborhood** of French Hill, Bobby, told me he had started building a raft on Fort Pond. This interested me so I volunteered to help him finish it and take it out onto the lake. Fort Pond is located in Lancaster and is named after the nearby Army base: Fort Devens. At that time the shore was dotted with summer cottages or what we called "camps." Bobby had begun the raft in a small clearing near the lake at the end of a long path through the woods. We hid our bikes at the entrance to the path and walked in. Soon we began finishing off this cobbled-together pile of scrap wood and branches. Pathetic as it looked, I had visions of us pushing it off and poling along the lake's surface like a pair of modern-day Huckleberry Finns.

As we readied to launch, I noticed that I had been hearing a buzzing sound that was growing louder. I looked down and saw that it was coming from a little hole in the ground—Yellow jackets in a ground hive. We had repeatedly stomped up and down the path near the hive and a few bees were now hovering around its entrance in an agitated state.

"Hey Bobby, I think we're bugging these bees," I said, to which he answered with one of the great *clichés.*

"They won't bother us if we don't bother them."

Finally we were finished. We grabbed our poles and shoved off from the shore. However we *had* apparently bugged the bees because once we were out only a few yards they swarmed us. Bees were everywhere, their buzzing now a roar, stinging us everywhere they could. We windmilled our arms, yelled and screamed in pain but they kept at it. There was no choice but to abandon ship. We dove into the pond, swimming away from the raft underwater with stinging bees still stuck to our bodies. I lifted my head to fill my lungs and they were swarming over me waiting to pounce.

At last we were far enough away that they were behind us. We dragged ourselves onto the shore, still pulling the little bastards off. Bobby said we should put mud on the stings—a poultice of sorts—which we did and the pain seemed to subside.

&

*Coda:*

*I learned a hard lesson about bees that day, but in retrospect, they probably saved my life. I'm not much of a swimmer and that was not much of a raft.*

*Mechanic and Water Streets—portals to French Hell*

# THE PLASTIC CITY

**Location**

**Leominster** (LemonSTUH) is a city in Worcester (WisTAH) County, Massachusetts in the United States of America. Some 40,000-plus souls reside there, making it second-in-size to the County Seat of Worcester itself. It's located north of that city about an hour drive west from Boston. Both Routes 2 and 12 pass through, and I-190, 13, and 117 start and end there too. Fitchburg, Lunenburg, Lancaster, Sterling, Princeton and Westminster are its neighbors.

Leominster and Fitchburg are sometimes referred to as the "Twin Cities" because of their similar industrial backgrounds, populations and proximities to the Nashua (NASHway) river. In the 1890s the F&L Street Railway bought a swath of land in Lunenburg next to Lake Whalom and extended their tracks to what became Whalom Park—which was modelled along the lines of an English trolley park—where the line could entice riders to use their service on weekends. This triad is sometimes referred to as "Tri-Town."

❧

## History

Before the arrival of settlers from England, the Pennacook and Nipmuc tribes inhabited the land. Leominster was first settled in 1653 as part of the town of Lancaster, and the settlers lived there in close proximity and peace with Native Americans until the outbreak of King Phillip's War in 1675. During that conflict, most of Lancaster's inhabitants evacuated. Once the fighting had ceased, the settlement was left a virtual ghost town. In an effort to bring them back, a new grant of land (containing what is now Leominster and Sterling) was offered to the former occupants. To avoid further hostilities with the tribes, a negotiation with Chief Sholan of the Nashaway tribe resulted in one of the only pieces of land in Central Massachusetts to be legally purchased from them.

The first house was built in 1724 and by 1740 Leominster had gained enough citizens to be officially incorporated into a town and then a city in 1915 and was named after a city in England. The early town consisted of typical family farms.

The Plastic City was a major player in the Underground Railroad movement, and the Emory Stearn Schoolhouse and John Drake home figured prominently into anti-slavery efforts by helping shelter escaped slaves on their journey to freedom in Canada.

❧

## The Plastics Industry

Although the plastics industry in Leominster is but a shadow of its former self, it remains "The Pioneer Plastics City" due to its once-prodigious plastics industry plus its position as innovation-leader during the early part of the 20th century. The city has played a more significant role in the establishment and progress of plastics than any other in the world.

The plastics industry started with comb making in the

1770s and has flourished ever since. Early combs were made of animal shells, horns, and hooves, but by the mid-19th century, supplies were dwindling as demand increased. In 1868, John Wesley Hyatt invented a material made from Cellulose Nitrate which he dubbed "Celluloid." It was hard, durable and easy to shape when heated to the proper temperature.

With that, local facilities for horn fabrication transformed into plastic manufacturing shops. Its factories used Celluloid not only for combs but also for toys, cutlery handles, glasses frames, buttons and novelties. Most Celluloid manufacturing was later changed to Cellulose Acetate which was less flammable.

The peak of the industry was between 1900 and 1920 when it was the city's largest employer.

&

**Author's note:**

*Leominster is also the birthplace of the pink flamingo lawn ornament, the street hockey puck, Foster Grant sunglasses AND Johnny Appleseed!* **Top that world.**

*French Hill*

# MY VIEW

**In my youth, Leominster was** a small factory town alongside a dirty river called the Nashua. The river got that way with the advent of the Industrial Revolution when it was used as an open sewer by all of the mills upstream. It often changed color depending upon which pigments were being used in the making of paper in Fitchburg. It could be a wide variety of pastels but most days it was a light, milky grey. The Nashua served as our outer boundary, although we did cross it now and then...*carefully*. There is now a shopping mall built on its floodplain but when we ran there, it was like a wide-open African savannah.

If you walked along the shore and looked down, you would see that the pulp in the water from the paper mills had hardened leaving a crust of a kind of cardboard something like a grey egg carton. If you poked a hole in that crust with your toe, you revealed a shoreline that was covered with the pristine white beach sand that once squished between the toes of our Indian forbears.

*Victory Button summer outing, early-1950s*

# PLASTIC

**If you climbed up the sides** of the canyon formed over eons by the Nashua, you would find yourself on one of the numbered streets of French Hill. They ran one through 12 and were intersected by Mechanic, Spruce, Laurel and Water streets forming a grid. There was a disorganized lozenge of land created by the awkward flow of streets that ended in a no-mans'-land called Wells Court. In my fertile imagination, the "Court" reminded me of the plaza in front of the Cathédrale Notre Dame de Paris where the drama of *The Hunchback of Notre Dame* played out. It was something about the way you looked up at St. Cecelia's Church from the rear, where it stood imperially on the higher ground. It was like looking at "Our Lady of Paris" from the *Pont de l'Archevêché* that crosses the Seine.

French Hill got its nickname because of all the French-Canadians who had immigrated there to work in the plastic factories. They lived in three-decker tenements or modest homes like the one I grew up in. "The Hill" may not have been on the preferred side of the tracks in the minds of many, but it did have that jewel for its working-class crown—its church.

My family were not French-Canadians however. My stepfather was Italian and my mother was Irish. Both of their parents had come to America from their respective old countries. The father of my stepfather, Michele Tata, dislodged the family's Buick from the garage in back of his house on Sixth Street, installed a plastic injection molding machine and dubbed the enterprise the Victory Button. These were days when many companies were using "victory" in their names to sound more patriotic (especially those owned by recent immigrants).

With that this newly-minted entrepreneur started pumping out buttons and combs. The Victory Button factory replaced the garage and eventually expanded until it fronted Seventh Street.

By the time I came along, Michele had passed away and the plant—now called Tamor Plastics—was in a much larger facility on Carter Street (on French Hill but close to the Italian section near St. Ann's church). The operation was then being run by my stepfather, Anthony (Tony) and his brother Domenic (Dom). They were banging out hairbrushes, laundry baskets, novelty items and employing a lot of people.

*Plastics workers*

# INJECTION MOLDING

**If you had a job running** a molding machine you came
in at seven a.m. (the day shift) and stood next to a hulking
electrically-powered machine for the next eight hours. The
machine's main job was to push two halves of a mold together
under intense pressure. The molds had the halves of products
carved into them like the fossils of, let's say, combs. One half
of the mold went on one side of a platen and the other on the
other platen (the molds were changed when a new product was
called for).

The machine melted plastic pellets into a liquid state and
fed it into the mold halves after they'd slammed together.
Water was applied to the molds with tubing to cool the plastic
to perfection. Too little heat (too cool) and you got a "short;" a
product that was not fully formed such as in a comb with teeth
missing. A "flash" was caused by the plastic being too liquid
because of too much heat, thus creating excess plastic webbing
on the product.

Once this all happened, the mold yawned, the operator would open a safety gate, reach in and grab the combs on their stems and then close the gate which automatically slammed the mold shut thus beginning a new cycle of a minute or two. During this relaxing interlude, the operator lit a cigarette and busied himself/herself by breaking the combs off of the stems, inspecting for shorts and flashes and discarding the flawed ones along with the stems into a noisy grinder. The ground plastic would eventually make its way back into a machine's "hopper" to be melted again. The operator then packed the good combs into a box that sat on a scale. When the box weighed enough, a floor boy wheeled it away and left another empty box to replace it. From there it went to the shipping dock. A person had to stay up with the molding machine because if it stayed open too long it affected the temperature of the mold. If they could find that sweet spot in the timing they were a considered a good operator.

There were other skills at play in a plastic shop, but the essence of plastic manufacturing was that of an operator standing at a hot, noisy, smoky machine for eight hours trying to keep up with it so that all the temperatures were right and the company made its quota. When the temperatures went awry however, it might be necessary to reach in and clear a gob of plastic off the face of the mold. The machines were not supposed to close when the gates were open but sometimes they did. Should it close at wrong moment there was a red button to push that would force the machine's platens to reopen. I knew someone when I was in the shops who had to do this while two fingers and a thumb were stuck in the mold. He calmly pushed the red button and dislodged what was left of his right hand and then went about arranging a trip to Leominster Hospital. He wore the battle scar as a badge of duty but also a reminder to use care. Molding didn't pay well either, but when you just plain *needed* a job, you could usually find one doing it. In fairness, a lot of people were good at it and took pride in it— but it took a strong mind set.

*172 Ninth Street, Leominster, Massachusetts, 1950s*

# RITUAL

**Each December 29th** for many years now I have been making a pilgrimage back to the place in which I grew up—Leominster, Massachusetts and its environs. I usually have time off during this period and I set aside this day for the purpose of visiting my mother's final resting place which is actually in neighboring Fitchburg where she was raised. It is a workday today and the wet roads are noticeably under-traveled in the light drizzle. The weather is warm for this time of year and fog rises from the melting snow making the trees look like pen and ink strokes against a cool grey wash along the highway: Winter in Massachusetts.

This year I'm driving west on Route 2—the Mohawk Trail—although I have altered my path in previous years in order to meander home off of the main highway through the little towns that constituted the stomping grounds of my youth to pick at the scattered remains of reminiscence. Many of my memories are well-worn and I can conjure them any time at all. But others blindside then astonish me with minutia about such things as the names of my friends' dogs (Rusty, Sparky, King and Rex). On these occasions mine come flooding in, grey as the Nashua or as luminous as auroras—the good, the bad and the ugly. And I open myself to all of it, for in addition to laying poinsettias at my mother's grave, the pursuit of those memories is why I make the drive.

My mother always had poinsettias around our house at Christmas. It was one of the few true rituals that we followed—that and geraniums for the dead on Memorial Day. She was born into a large Irish-Catholic family and needless to say that her birthday on this date did not garner a lot of attention coming as it did right after the holidays. I always think of that at this time of year.

I pull off the highway at the Arena Farm Stand in Concord to buy them. Their season is over and I'm the only customer in the shop. The girl behind the counter points me toward a table with a few leftover poinsettias in plastic pots gaily wrapped in red tin foil. They all look pretty drab but I grab two—one to take home to live and one to die in the cold. I pay with cash and the girl drops the chump change into my hand without looking at me.

I enter the rotary near Concord Prison and head west listening to oldies. Every *sha-la-la-la,* every *whoa-oo-oh-oh* tripping a synapse. Descending from a crest I spot Mount Wachusett and Saint Cecelia's Church. I pass Fort Devens, Spec Pond and Fort Pond—all settings for my childhood exploits and take the exit for Mechanic Street.

For the first time there are historical markers scattered around my old town. One is at the foot of Rice Hill which is long and steep but outside of the fact that a lot of us nearly killed ourselves biking down its slope has no historical significance that I know of. At the bottom is a road leading up to the birthplace of Johnny Appleseed.

*Ritual*

I cross the Nashua which is miraculously no longer the grey murk of my younger days but rather clean beyond all recognition. There is even a sign at Ninth and Mechanic streets denoting French Hill. Ninth Street at the bottom of the East Side Bus Loop is the gateway to "The Hill," and it's where once I lived—at number 172 with my mother Helen and my father, Tony Tata.

As always I drive slowly by the house looking for differences. I circle the block it's on—Ninth, Gordon, Tenth, Vezina. Actually I don't know what I'm looking for. Neither do I know if I want to be recognized or not. I'm not about to knock on the door but I always fantasize that someday I will see someone outside and get into a conversation about my having lived there and that they might invite me in to look inside for "old times' sake" and I would spout cliches such as, "It seems so much smaller than I remember."

*Hampton Beach*

# TRUDY AND MOE

**Trudy and Moe** were my second set of parents. I called them aunt and uncle but we were not related through blood. Trudy was Moe's German war bride. They had met while he was serving in the Navy during WWII. She had a singer's speaking voice and a sweet nature whose default facial expression was a half-smile. Through the lens of her perception she saw the glass as half-full—but she never gave you anything but the truth.

Their house on Ashburnham Street in West Fitchburg—where it claws north towards New Hampshire—frequently rang with her melodious voice on songs like "My Heart Cries for You," her favorite. Like my parents, they both were crazy about music.

Moe did something that involved trucks and his work clothes smelled deliciously of axle grease and Lucky Strikes when upon his arrival the kitchen would swing into action. He was possessed of an easygoing humor—but like his bride—he only spoke in *vēritātēs*. He was also funny and always seeking an opportunity for a laugh which he seemed to find everywhere.

Trudy had become acquainted with my mother's family through Saint John's Church. She had monitored the pregnancy and dispensed mothering advice with the wisdom born of experience. When I finally did come along, she was enchanted. Here was that Teutonic-looking, chubby, blue-eyed blond boy who must have looked like an infant figurine from a Hummel catalog.

My mother had not nailed down a suitable name for me as yet but was leaning towards Barry. Trudy kept tickling my chin as I lay in my carriage after Mass and calling me Janny (which sounded like Yunny the way she said it with her German accent). This evolved into Johnny and since everyone seemed to like it—and since it honors my mother's late brother—Johnny it would be.

The early years of my parents' marriage were sort of a prolonged honeymoon and as such, called for some child-free time. Thus by mutual accord, I was often taken under the waiting wings of Trudy and Moe—sometimes for weeks on end. I may not have been pleased with this arrangement, but once there, I settled in and blended with their two sons: older Tommy (fair-haired, favoring his German mother) and David (dark-haired like Italian Moe). The boys may not have invited another rival for mother's attention, but although David exhibited a chip on his shoulder from time-to-time, Tommy—on the high road to his Eagle Scout badge—never let things get too far out of hand. I spent so much time in their toast and cocoa-scented kitchen that I began calling Trudy "Ma" the way her own boys did, and Tommy and David became like my own brothers.

❧

Moe and Trudy liked to take the tribe out for a joyride in their shiny silver Chevy on Sundays (it was grey, but Trudy preferred to call the color silver), and this usually included ice cream and picnic tables.

On the way back to West Fitchburg after one such outing, "Cross over the Bridge" by Patti Page was playing on the car radio. This was a perplexing time in American pop culture because once there was Elvis, there was also Rock and Roll. Both seemed to arrive simultaneously. A genre could not start with one person (could it?), and folks conjectured as to the origin of this seemingly radical music. Patti Page had been hugely successful for years leading up to the advent of Rock and Roll and some people thought that her rendition of "Bridge" with its (for that time) hard backbeat may have actually been the opening salvo of this new musical onslaught.

&#9880;

Once Tommy and David tired of playing with the family's newest game from the variety store I got a chance at it. It was called *Wooly Willy*. The game was a typical low-tech toy of its time—a little something to keep a young mind occupied for a short while on a long ride. It consisted of a piece of hard cardboard imprinted with a bald, clean-shaven cartoon man whom I suppose was Willy. The cardboard was encased in a hard plastic blister-pack and came with magnet. Inside the blister-pack were packets of lead balls the size of birdshot.

The game was that you could drag gobs of the birdshot around with the "Magic Wand" magnet and drop it onto Willy's face and head, giving him mustaches, sideburns (like Elvis), a beard perhaps or…

…the atmosphere became electric in the car. A low but insistent roar seemed to be coming from behind. Tommy and David were on their knees on the backseat staring back down Route 2. Trudy looked back amusedly over her left shoulder as she idly toyed with the back of Moe's hair and I could see his eyes looking back in the rear-view mirror.

Motorcycles—a dozen or so—were converging on us like a squadron of *Focke-Wulf 190s* (right out of Moe's collection of Wings cigarette collector's cards) from six o'clock high. A large one pulled alongside the car in passing. Although my window was closed, the throaty roar of its engine was deafening.

The motorcycle had a sort of windshield on the front mounted to the handlebars and sported an Indian chief in a full headdress on the gas tank. The rider was wearing a visored captain's cap which would have made him look like a military commander if not for being black with white trim. He wore a black leather jacket with an arcane assortment of zippers.

Glancing at the passengers in the Chevy, he smirked and then shouted something over his shoulder to the woman clinging to him from behind his back in a love embrace. Talking caused his Adam's apple to piston visibly under the stubble of his craned neck.

His passenger was perched on the bike's huge saddle which appeared to be covered with royal-blue shag carpeting. Her hair was covered with a kerchief knotted fussily under her delicate, birdlike jaw. She too wore a multi-zippered leather jacket but it was a feminized version with white trim on the belt, pocket tops, collar and *epaulets*. She rotated her big, black cat's-eye sunglasses towards the car and gave me a turn by actually seeming to peer in at me—but when she groomed her lipsticked lips by licking them, I suspected that she might have just been looking at her own reflection fleeting by on the sheen of the car window.

The bikes roared past us one-by-one, each upshifting and peeling off in a signature way like it was taking a bow. Some had women passengers, some did not. There were similarities in what they rode and what they wore but not one was exactly the same as any other. Then they were gone, disappearing north towards Gardner.

&

*Coda:*

*No one noticed that the littlest passenger in the Chevy—the quiet, toe-headed one—had been transformed...irrevocably.*

*Jimmy and me*

# CONCORD ROTARY

**Jimmy and I had been** hitchhiking our way to Boston and were dropped off by our first ride at the Concord rotary near the prison. We had just started walking when we heard a crunching sound from behind. It was a state trooper cruiser following slowly on the soft shoulder. We tried to pretend it wasn't there for as long as we could but we soon found ourselves inside the car. The State Police barracks was conveniently located directly across Route 2 from the prison gate. We were wearing white T-shirts and dungarees just like the inmates in the adjacent farm field and the officer took us in because he thought we might have walked away from a work detail.

Once inside they could see that we were not old enough to be in the prison but they had us empty our pockets anyway 'cause...that's what cops do. As they watched, we threw the contents onto a scarred old wooden table with "book you" incised all over the top. Jimmy was carrying a lot so he created quite a pile for himself. I was only carrying a pocket comb and I remember the trooper commenting wryly to me, "You travel light, don't you?"

We wouldn't be going to Boston that day as it turned out. The officer called Jimmy's father to come and pick us up. His dad was kind of a strict guy but he just made a joke out of it on this day. After all—we hadn't really done anything—you know—wrong. On the way home he got a big kick out of driving by my house and seeing my mother on the front porch with a broom. "You're in for it now," he said laughingly, but in fact my mother hadn't heard anything from anybody. That she was sweeping the porch was merely a coincidence. I still had not broken her "**Just Don't Come Home In A Cruiser**" rule.

&#8494;

*Coda:*

*And what had been the reason for this little jaunt to the big city? Why—it was to buy a budding juvenile delinquent's must-have accessory—a push-button switchblade knife. I had it in my head that they sold them at Jack's Joke Shop in Park Square along with the masks and the rubber vomit.*

*Ersatz Brando*

# RED RYDER

**At foot of the valley wall** was a fire road and then a stream. The stream's proper name was Monoosnock Brook but everybody on French Hill called it the Little Nashway (Nashua) after its larger counterpart in the middle of the valley. It meandered though the floodplain for a few miles and then emptied into the grey Nashua proper.

The Little Nashway was an obstacle that needed to be contended with when negotiating that particular patch of woods. It could be six to 18-feet-across and not very deep but over your head in places which could vary with the weather.

We had our places to cross—narrow sections, fallen trees, trash boards and the like—but these could be unpredictable. If you didn't want to risk getting wet, you had to walk back to Whitney Field which was quite a distance.

One winter day three of us approached the stream: Bobby, Frankie and I. We'd been shooting our BB guns out on the big

Nashua's snow-covered floodplain but now the sun was going down, the light was dimming and the air grew colder. We were heading for French Hill, but first we had to cross the Little Nashway. Luckily it was frozen so we could simply walk across. We would do so with an abundance of caution though, one at a time. Frankie went first. There was an ominous low groan and some crickling sounds that made him pause for a second in the middle but then he hustled off the ice—safe on the far side and looking back. "Come on," he coaxed.

They tried to get me to cross next but I was not convinced about the safety of that ice, even though I was the youngest of the three and therefore the lightest. Eventually Bobby got tired of waiting for me and started across cradling the Red Ryder air rifle that I'd always admired. He was huskier than skinny curly-headed Frankie, and suddenly a hole in ice opened under him just big enough for him to fall through. He barely had time to yell. He went under then his head bobbed up gasping with his hair in his face like he'd gone swimming. The current was taking him with it and he was swept to the edge of the breach then his head went under again.

For a second it seemed like he was gone completely and Frankie and I gaped at the hole in shock. Then Frankie noticed that Bobby's hands were still showing. They were hanging on to the edge, trying desperately to keep himself from going downstream under the ice. Frankie started making his way out onto the ice taking little ice-skating steps. I expected to see him fall in too, but the ice held. It was like that stream wanted Bobby; not him. He made his way over to Bobby's hands and lying down, starting pulling—the hands and then the arms. Bobby's head came out and Frankie managed to get a grip under his armpits and also enough traction to pull him out. They were struggling but in a very controlled way—if that makes any sense.

Bobby and Frankie got off of the ice, both of them shaken. They were on the French Hill side of the Little Nashway and

*Red Ryder*

I wasn't, and they looked at me once, then without speaking headed towards the side of the valley wall and home. I'd be taking the long way back via Whitney Field.

&

*Coda:*

*The Red Ryder was taken by the stream where I assume some rusted remnant of it still rests. It had a wooden stock (not like the plastic one of my Daisy) and a ring that had a strip of rawhide tied to it—an Indian brave's rifle. Little braves like us. Like in the movies.*

*Open me first*

# THE CAVE

**Somehow, through some mysterious** grapevine or tribal drumbeat, word had come down that there existed nearby, a cave ripe for exploring. Caves were a *leitmotif* of movies and television in those days, promising action, adventure and mystery—an irresistible kid magnet. The location of the cave was off our normal turf as I remember so it was probably in Lancaster or Shirley, a pretty fair distance. Since it was said to be in a wooded area, we left our bikes at home and "hoofed it" instead. We trekked to what we'd heard was the general location of the site and then cut though a wooded patch that opened up into a clearing in front of a near-vertical rock-faced cliff.

The place was buzzing with activity. Kids I didn't know were leaving, arriving…and crawling in and out of a little opening at the base of the cliff like ants. There was excited chattering about cave experiences all around us. No adult supervision here. No cops, no firemen, no priests, no nuns, no teachers, no lifeguards and no parents. There were no ropes, no lights, no fences, no cars, no phones and no admission tickets. Whoever I was with, maybe Johnny or Jimmy, saw his turn come around and he dropped down and low crawled into the opening armed only with a flashlight. After 10 or 15 minutes he popped back out exhilarated.

"It's cool," he said, catching his breath, "you crawl in for a while then you come to a big cave that you can stand up in. Then you can turn around and crawl out."

"What's in there?" I asked.

"Nothing much," he said, "just some old campfire charcoal and some writing on the walls."

"How far in is it?" I wondered.

"Not far," he said so...

...with some reservations, I got down and scrabbled into the opening, flashlight in hand. On my hands and knees to begin but soon crawling I made my way through the tunnel. As I did, I felt the opening become small and then smaller still. I was in a good 14 feet when I rested and shined the light ahead of me panting. No larger cave could be seen, just more tunnel.

In the silence and gloom I became aware of my quickening breathing and heartbeat. I had a fleeting impulse to bail out but I didn't want to seem chicken. Not to mention that I was also still curious about the cave, so deeper in I went. But in a few more feet I snagged completely and couldn't move forward any further. Once more I pointed the flashlight up the tunnel but still couldn't make out any cave, and I began to wonder exactly *how* far in it really was.

Maybe I was fatter than the other guys who were doing this crawl but all I knew was that *I* was now stuck, and I was starting to get *very* nervous. Once I'd had enough I started trying to back out but at first I couldn't move that way either. Now the situation was getting serious indeed. I needed to give myself a good firm talking to in order to keep from going into a complete panic. There was going to be no way to get out of this hole if I didn't. There would be no rescue trucks coming in the nick of time, just some sad little story on the news at six or in the *Leominster Enterprise* along with my school picture, I'd imagined. I tried to shift around a little and finally with effort managed to purchase a little wiggle room. Little-by-little I freed myself from the grip of the tunnel. With painful slowness I inched out backward. Crawling in reverse was a much slower process than crawling forward I was discovering.

&

*Coda:*

*After what seemed like an eternity, I emerged from my would-be tomb into that brilliant summer sunshine. I would have liked to have told my friend that I had gone all the way in just to save face, but he'd seen my feet come out first so that would have been pretty hard to fake. And with that my spelunking days came and went.*

*Geno, Zeke, Andy and James Dean (oh wait, that's me)*

# GALAXY 500

**One of my running buddies** early in my 17th year was a kid named Gregg. We were in the same class at LHS but didn't share classes. Gregg was a somewhat eccentric but genial guy with a great sense of absurdest humor. Like me, he identified as a "Packrat." Packrat was a term given to what now might be called a "Greaser" and was specific to the Fitchburg/Leominster area. It was gradually shortened to the much more manageable "Rat" or "Packy."

Rats liked the image of the 1950s teenaged hoodlum and emulated their manner, mode of dress and hairstyle—bikers without bikes (what the British would call Teddy Boys). Where that moniker came from I can't say, but I do know that the name for our nemeses, the "Lunchies," had something to do with the Fitchburg Luncheonette. They favored a collegiate look: bucks, white socks, khakis and madras shirts—surfers without surf.

Under the influence of the Beatles, I was beginning to degrease. One illustration of my difficulty in making this transition would be my process of getting my senior class picture made. In the first proofs my hair is slicked up into a James Dean/Elvis Presley pompadour. I nixed those because my hairline was already receding. In the second set you get Lennon/McCartney. My hair wasn't quite long enough to pull that off so it was a no-go as well. Net result: no picture. If you get hold of a 1966 Leominster High School yearbook there will be no formal portrait of me—however, I can be seen slouching in the top row of the Art Club photo, Beatle-banged to beat the band.

We were trying to form bands in those days and I was working out songs with my friend Ray on bass guitar and me strumming chords on my noodle-necked Eglund guitar. We even had a name for it—the "Teddy Boys." We didn't have a drummer but it turned out that Gregg played a bit and owned a drum kit, which was prerequisite *numero uno*. One memorable evening he picked us up in his father's big black and chrome Ford Galaxy and drove us to his house to practice. Judging by Gregg's home, the family must have been wealthy. It was huge—a mansion really—at the end of a long driveway at the top of a wooded hill near Whalom Park. It was like a scene from a horror movie driving up the long, white gravel driveway in thunder and lightning and then having that enormous, mostly dark house come looming into view.

He gave us the obligatory house tour that everyone seems to give. There was a classical symphony blaring from an upstairs room which blared even louder when Gregg opened the study door to introduce us to his older brother whom we found standing in the middle of the room conducting the recorded music. He was waving a baton to the rhythm with one hand while brandishing a pitcher of martinis in the other which he swigged from when he turned around. His eyes and hair were wild and although he seemed to register our presence, it was only faintly. We left him alone and went to do our own musical thing which turned out to be pretty awful. We taped a little and I found that I could sound a bit like John Lennon which I suppose was the evening's high spot.

⨕

## When the Galaxy Rolls Over

One sunny Sunday not long after that we were joy-riding in the Galaxy when Gregg took a notion to scare the shit out of me so, rather than take the normal route to Whalom Park via Main Street, he cut right onto little-used Day Street and stomped on the gas. The big V-8 lurched into overdrive and the acceleration pushed me into my seat.

Day Street was just wide enough for two cars to get past each other with slightly more caution than normal. The street had a cow pasture bordered by a New England stone fence on the driver's side, while on the passenger's side there was a steep hill that came right down to the road. As we rounded a curve there was a milk truck lumbering up towards us straddling the white line. There was no time to stop, we were going to hit it, so Gregg yanked the wheel to the right and drove the car up onto the embankment. The speed and the angle began to flip the car and as it did, Gregg reached over and tried to push me into my seat by the shoulder to no avail. The Galaxy landed on its roof and slid about 20 yards down the street beyond the milk truck. There were no seat belts and I hit the head liner. As I did the dirt from the mats and the breaking safety glass hit me in face but I was fortunate to be wearing sunglasses which protected my eyes.

Suddenly it got all quiet. I crawled out of the window stunned, cutting my hands on the glass and assessed the situation. I figured I was all right because nothing hurt and outside of my hands nothing was bleeding. I looked at the car tracks cut into the hillside. They ended where the wheels had left the ground. It was obvious that had the car not flipped we would have smashed into a telephone pole (Gregg later insisted that the flip was done intentionally to avoid the pole). He had scrambled out and was unscathed as well—already fretting about his next conversation with his father. The milkman directed me down the street to warn any oncoming vehicles that the way was blocked. Nobody came for a while so after I got bored I hitchhiked back to downtown Leominster.

My hair was getting kind of long so I went into the barbershop where my friend Andy worked. He had gone to barbering school and was apprentice to the shop's Master-Barber owner. Andy wasn't a particularly good barber, but he loved to gab which is an asset in that profession. It's only natural that the barber/patron patter centered on my adventure of that morning. Andy kept pulling shards of safety glass out of my hair as he combed it, laughing in amazement. Whoa!

After the Galaxy rolled over, Gregg dropped off my radar. Despite my cavalier attitude following the accident, I was well aware that he had damn near killed me showing off.

Some time later, he approached me about borrowing my motorcycle jacket. He had *"frankensteined"* a "chopper" of sorts from parts of other bikes, and he wanted my leather for safety and—you know—"*coolth.*" I didn't know who he was trying to impress nor did I care. That chapter was ending for me and it was time to be moving on.

&

## Death of a Wild One

Up until that time though, my leather jacket had meant a great deal to me indeed. After seeing *The Wild One* at the Plymouth Theater with my mother in what must have been 1954, I wanted one in the worst way. That image of Brando leading B.R.M.C. up a highway was etched into my psyche, driven home by the fact that his character in film was named Johnny. My mother was less than fond of that image for her little boy, and a prolonged test of wills ensued. She detested motorcycles as well, referring to them as "death cars." Through negotiations, a series of jackets were purchased that were "close-

*34*

but-no-cigar." Those served to hold my *holy grail* at bay until five years later when she finally relented and bought me that iconic garment—my mantle of the *Rebel Hero*.

It came from a shop downtown and one night when I got home, she surprised me with it. In my mind's eye I can still see it folded in its gift box. The supple leather, the silvery trim and that *smell*. It was the most luxurious thing that I'd ever seen up close.

Looking back, that jacket colored my adolescence and probably not in the best way possible. I was warned early on that it would attract trouble and trouble did seem to find me. We do what we do I guess.

*Coda:*

*In the end, my Wild One went out in a blaze of glory. Gregg had been riding his Frankenchopper when a dog jumped out and pulled him off his ride. Although he was unhurt (lucky once again), the bike, and the jacket were totalled. He returned it to me in tatters and I threw what was left of it away.*

*In recounting this story, two thoughts occur to me. First: Gregg's accident was the only time the jacket was ever atop a motorcycle. Second: I'm glad that I had not been wearing it at the time.*

*Nana*

# KNOCKMANAGH

**This is a picture of my Grandmother**, Hannah Gallagher, when she was a recent immigrant from Ireland. The inscription on the back says that it was taken in 1911 when she was 19-years-of-age. When I was small, I would sometimes stay at her house on Sprague Street in West Fitchburg, Massachusetts. My Grandpa had passed away and once her youngest, Robert, moved away, she was alone. She lived in a compact two-story Victorian with a *Mansard* roof. Although the house had updated plumbing, the original well pump was still in the kitchen.

Her Aunt Mag had once occupied the house, but by this time she had moved up to the second floor and that became her own apartment. I can just remember her from my earliest days. It was perennially underlit up there and Aunt Mag seemed so terribly small and frail, wizened and brown as the WWII souvenir coconut Nana kept in her parlour. Mag really seemed to love me though and when I would visit along with my cousins Paula and her brother Diggy, she would practically straight-arm them out of the way to draw me to her side. Or so it seemed.

I remember two things that my mother told me about this pious Catholic woman. Ma was amazed at how "saintly" Aunt Mag would drown unwanted kittens in a bucket of water, and also that how at the end of her life; she had pleaded that—even at her advanced age—death not come for her. Those memories are what I have left of Aunt Mag. That along with a sepia photograph and some *Blue Willow* china marked "Buffalo, 1906."

Both stories had belonged to Mag and her husband John McGowan, but once Nana took over the first floor, the unused inside staircase to the second floor eventually became clogged with shoes, wooden golf clubs, sleds and clothes on hangers to the point of being virtually impenetrable. Yet in the way of the child, I spelunked my way through in my explorations. I used to have nightmares about clawing my way up there but once upstairs, panicking and trying to get back down in a hurry to escape some nameless entity.

Nana's house had flowered wallpaper of an antique design, its grim bulbous blossoms threatened to devour any child that came too close. It made it hard to sleep knowing that they were there on the walls...*watching*. The light switches were of the button type—one for off one for on—and the old bulbs seemed to give up their dim wattage grudgingly. Grandpa's leather razor strop still hung in the bathroom (used for corporal punishment as well a razor sharpening—or so went the legend). I marveled at a pair of gallstones that decorated Nana's bookcase (her own). Whatever art was on the walls was of the religious variety (Jesus with a flock of sheep or the Blessed Virgin's beatific face—prayerful hands laced with rosary beads).

There was one photo of her parents in an oval mahogany frame with convex glass staring down from the wall—her father sporting a handlebar moustache and a dubious expression. Later on; the famous Bachrach photographic portrait of John

F. Kennedy would grace her parlor as it did in so many Irish-American homes—but there I'm getting ahead of myself.

Television was not a factor in that house and most of the time I spent there was in talking with Nana at the kitchen table over tea and toast (made in a toaster that did one side at a time). She'd tell me stories about all her 11 children and ones about Ireland—the "Ould Sod" as she called it, in the charming Irish lilt that she never lost. What follows is one of them.

&

**An Capall (The Horse)**
Back when she was a young girl in Knockmanagh, her family had fallen on hard times. They desperately needed cash and decided to sell the only "luxury" they could live without—their horse. So one day her father bridled it and headed for the big city to sell it. It was a long trip that necessitated sleeping-in-the-rough. Upon awakening the next morning of this journey, her father awoke to find the poor beast had died during the night. So that it would not be a total loss, he made the decision to skin it and then to proceed to the city to sell the hide for leather.

He was well into this grisly process when, to his astonishment, *the horse revived, stood up and whinnied—flaps of skin hanging off of its sides like the grotesque wings of a nightmare Pegasus.* In a panic, he immediately began to cut little twigs from the surrounding bushes and sharpen their ends. He pressed the sections of skin back into place and secured them with these "pins." It wasn't pretty but the skin held. No one was going to be interested in the animal in this condition so he walked the poor thing home.

&

*Coda:*
*I asked Nana if the horse had been okay and she said yes, the skin grafted back to its body, but, that the following spring, tiny branches with leaves began to sprout out of the horse's sides where the pins had been. This she told me with her patented deadpan delivery.*

39

*Me and Geno*

# NIGHT GAMES

**I never played Football** in high school. I did go to some of the games but it was more about hanging around, seeing and trying to be seen, horseplay and chasing girls around, and of course, we always went in over the fence. I never paid much attention to the games, truth be told, but they always seemed to be played on the most beautiful days of the fall, crisp and sunny. One of the Blue Devils rivals during the season back then was the Nashua High School team: the Panthers. This was an away game, up in New Hampshire and it was kind of exciting because it was a night game, played under the lights like the pros.

My crew, The Rebels, drove up to attend, probably in Ray's car because he was the only one with one at that time. Besides Ray there was Zeke, Geno, possibly Andy and me. We were wearing our Packrat gear: motorcycle jackets, dungarees, engineer boots and garrison belts. The belts were customized with chrome studs and we had heard that if you sharpened the buckles, they could be used as weapons in the unlikely event of a "rumble" so we did that too. This was in the early-Sixties but we looked like extras from the *The Wild One*. I had painted the Big Daddy Roth cartoon character "Rat Fink" on the backs of all of the jackets just to drive the point home that we were Rats and proud of it. When we walked into the stadium and climbed into the stands that night, I overheard someone say, "It wouldn't be a Leominster game without the Packrats." I felt so *proud*.

At halftime we went over to use the mens' room which was on the Nashua side. On the way back we were horseplaying around and at one point Geno pushed me from behind and I stumbled forward. This happened just as the Nashua team was returning to the field for the second half and I kind of ended up in the middle of them causing a little pileup. A Nashua cop pulled me up and pushed me out of the stadium. He had my arm bent behind my back and at one point he twisted it as hard as he could and looked at my face to see the pain. I just rolled my eyes in boredom which seemed to enrage him.

He bum-rushed me over to a police cruiser that was idling in the parking lot. "Take this punk to the station and book him," he said.

"We've already got a full load," the cop riding shotgun said, gesturing at a couple of inebriated Leominster teens in the back seat.

"Then let one go and take this one instead," said the first cop, and that's what they did. He stuck his head in though the window and sneered at me, "Take *good* care of him." Both the cop riding shotgun and the driver looked back over their shoulders at me. The kid sitting next to me was starting to sober off.

They brought me into the station and over to an old-fashioned wooden booking desk which looked like a teller's cage. While one cop asked questions and scribbled something down, I noticed behind him another was smiling lugubriously and making a gesture with his hands: his right fist pounding into his left palm. The way I took it was that I had been hauled in for getting into a fight. I sort of caught the cop behind me from the corner of my eye nodding his head and grinning in return.

This cop, who was a grown-up and much bigger than I was, pushed me toward the cells, but halfway there he stopped me in the hallway and punched me in that stomach with all that he had. Once I had buckled over he completed the combination with a good crack across the back of my head. With my welcome to Nashua ceremony now complete, he shoved me into a cell, slammed the gate, locked it and left.

&

While all of this was happening, Geno had made his way to the station. He burst through the doors demanding my release. Geno's father worked for the Leominster Police Department but Geno told the Nashua police that *our* father (he had made me his brother for this story) was the Chief of the LPD. Now why, dressed as he was, and what with the ruckus he was causing, they did not arrest him too I have no idea. Maybe they just let me go to shut him up, but the next thing I knew I was out of my cell and being led down a corridor towards the lobby. There were cops and lawyers lining the walls to see who was the cause of all this commotion and they might have been expecting John Dillinger by the way they were gawking at me.

&

Coda:

*Geno and I pushed open the big oak double-doors of the station house and hopped down the granite steps laughing in the face of the night—laughing at the silly moon. We headed south, bound for the Plastic City in Ray's finny old Ford convertible, not much worse for wear.*

*Dennis, Mike, Me and Chas*

# KATZENJAMMER KIDS

**During the winter of** 70–71 I made my living as a bassist/ singer with The Katzenjammer Kids. I'd joined the band soon after my somewhat halfhearted stab at the Art Institute of Boston. I was living in Brighton when I got a call from my old friend Dennis. He and I had played in a couple of bands over the years and had remained in touch after those had folded. He asked if I was staying in school and I told him no and that I'd be moving back to my parents' house in Leominster. He told me to dust off my old Fender Jazz Bass then because he had a spot for me in a new and as yet unnamed band.

Dennis had been playing his Hammond organ with a group that included lead guitarist Mike; whom I'd played in bands with in high school; a singer named Wayne that I knew from French Hill; and a drummer that I didn't named Chas. Wayne—who like me—played bass, was leaving the group thus creating an opening.

# The Boy from Plastic City

❦

I'd missed playing music that year in Boston, missed my hometown and that familiar music scene too and it was good to be going home and having a gig waiting for me. We got together a bit and worked out our repertoire. The group actually had ambitions to make money (novel approach *that* was) and we thought that to work better venues some sort of uniforms were in order which was a short-lived trend at that time. We drove into Cambridge and went to a *Mod* shop in Harvard Square called the Krackerjack and picked some corduroy jumpsuit/ overall-type things that fit tight and snapped up the front. Mike, Dennis and I got the mustard color and Chas got brown since that was all that was left. We picked up some matching shirts too—all the while flirting mercilessly with the salesgirls.

My mother came up with the name for the band based on the old comic strip of the same name. She helped us out again by chipping in on a van. It was an old Chevy Greenbriar, it's finish faded to a flat moss green. Since I was the artist, Dennis handed me a can of white paint and a brush one afternoon and had me write the name of the band all over it in my bubbly hippy lettering. In its own psychedelic way it was effective, and a sight to behold rattling up I-95 with us and our equipment crammed into it. One time we slept in it in a Salisbury Beach parking lot. When unamused cops woke us up in the morning they called us "gypsies" which we took as a compliment.

We played Micky's on the beach at Salisbury, and a frat party in Burlington, Vermont. There was a lifeguard end-of-season party at a hall where somebody broke a window and they *docked our pay to cover it!* We played a bar at an old hotel in Podunk where the owner loved the band but the feeling was not mutual so one night we just didn't show up (we got word later that he was going to break our thumbs and we were legitimately concerned). We played the Buttercup and the Fairmount Cafe, and we were the house band at the Three Copper Men in Lowell, six-nights-a-week, one winter, back in the day.

46

*Jimmy's brother Johnny played with guns*

# THE PHOENIX

*Prelude:*

*The love affair starts with caps. Caps are rolls of paper that have little charges of gunpowder affixed at regular intervals that fire inside of a kid's toy cap gun. Pull the trigger...bang. Pull the trigger...bang. It's not loud but it is satisfying. The gunpowder even smells good—kind of like incense. One of those smells like new tar, gas on a lake, mothballs or a skunk at a safe distance that shouldn't smell good but does. Now: if you take a whole cap roll out onto the street and drop a big rock on it, all the little charges go off at once and you get a major bang, much like a cherry bomb or even an M-80...**Bang**. You get a more consistent, louder bang if you whack it with a hammer, but you've got to remember to cover your cap-side ear with your free hand...**BANG**. This report could be heard for miles.*

❧

**Martin's mom-and-pop store** on Fifth Street had gotten

in a new novelty for us kids to enjoy: a dummy firecracker. The joke was; you put a fuse into a red cardboard canister that looked real, lit it and then threw it at your victim who would then run for his/her life. There would be no blast of course because the canister was devoid of powder. What interested us was not the joke, but the fuses. It was the real thing and we started buying up all that Martin's had and I'm guessing they needed to restock this hot item frequently.

At first we tried stuffing the dummy canisters with match heads but when the fuses burned down to the end, the match heads burned in an unsatisfying, dull way. David—who was a whiz kid at school—found a formula for gunpowder and actually mixed some up but the mixture was not right and once again there was more fizzle than bang.

⚬

One of our French Hill gang—probably Johnny—had disappeared into the trees one fall day and found his way onto the grounds of Fort Devens. He had wandered onto the field where the soldiers had their training maneuvers and found an eight-clip of .30 caliber rounds for M-1 rifles. The slugs had been removed and the powder sealed into the shells with little red pieces of cardboard. These were blanks, so that the soldiers could experience the illusion of combat without actually shooting one another. When he showed us the clip he told us that there was a lot more out there.

We packed one of our dummy firecrackers with the army powder from the blanks, lit the fuse and tossed it. It made a better explosion but the casing was not sealed well enough to compress the combustion and while it was an improvement, it was still no cigar. Mostly show and not much go.

⚬

Our appetites however had now been whetted and we embarked on a mission to gather some more discarded ordnance for, after all, if they didn't want it...? We negotiated our way onto the fort and then with Johnny's guidance, to the mock battlefield. There we found bunkers made from cut trees and it was extremely cool to be there for us army-playing French Hill kids. No one was around. Why they left so much ammo just laying there remains a mystery, but we just figured they didn't feel like carrying anything extra back to the base. We on the other hand were happy to clean up for them.

In addition to the M-1 clips, shells were clipped together into belts for feeding into the .30 cal. Machine guns—yards and yards of them in fact—hundreds of blank shells were scattered about and we filled our pockets. We'd hit the motherlode!

A couple of us wrapped the shells around our bodies like *Sergeant Rock of Easy Company* did in the comic books. It was all concealed by our coats but we must have looked pretty portly walking up Roller Coaster Road that overcast fall day. For good measure we had also grabbed a couple of aluminum-housed phosphorus flares because they looked cool and then route-stepped back to French Hill.

&

## Roller Coaster Road

We made our way up Roller Coaster Road in front of Spec Pond and Lancaster Beach. There were five of us walking single-file when the last man (boy) in the column said, "uh oh." A Lancaster police cruiser was coming slowly up behind us crunching the gravel of the soft shoulder. Jimmy's brother Johnny started singing the Ink Spots oldie "Up a Lazy River" which was French Hill slang for going to prison. Johnny had a penchant for gallows humor. The police stopped next to us and got out of the car.

It was all very friendly at first because we all appeared to be innocent young kids (if a little chubby), and the cops were genuinely nice guys. As stated, it was in the fall and the cop explained that there had been break-ins at some summer cottages on the lake and that they were checking us out for that reason. Once he looked at us I don't think he really suspected us of anything and they were about to move on when he noticed that Johnny was clutching something in the pocket of his jacket. A cop asked him what it was and Johnny held it out for him to see.

"Bullets," he blurted out, almost proudly I thought.

The officer grabbed the clip away from him and chided him for having them. Then he asked the rest of us had any. We knew we were busted so reluctantly we began opening our jackets and emptying out our pockets. The cops' mouths were agape. These chubby boys were armed to the teeth! He demanded that we give him whatever else we had and of course we complied (with most of it). They stacked the armaments in the backseat of the Crown Vic and there was enough of it so that the car tilted back a little on its suspension.

They took our names and we gave them—not our *real* names of course—but names nonetheless, and then they left. We stood in the road and watched them drive off, surprised that we weren't going to the station along with the swag. We counted our blessings and made our way to The Hill.

&

The following day, I thought I'd better do some damage control and see if there was anything about the incident in the *Leominster Enterprise*. I waylaid the paperboy on Eighth Street in front of my friend Freddy's house before he got to mine. The paperboy and I had been through this exercise on previous occasions so he knew the drill. I grabbed a paper and leafed through to page two. There was an article, a picture and a caption about what the Lancaster police had found. The picture showed the bullets stacked on a tarpaulin on the police station floor. Our names, fake as they may have been, were not mentioned, so I allowed the paperboy to deliver to our house.

&

Later, I had the guilty pleasure of hearing my mother comment on the story in the *Empty Prize*. "Imagine?" She had asked as she looked at the photograph and read the caption.

"I know," said I, innocent as a newborn lamb.

❧

## Phoenix Rising

Although the LPD had confiscated most of the liberated ammo, we still hung onto several of the .30 caliber M-1 clips hidden on our persons (dungaree pockets, socks et cetera). There was still enough powder to generate a pretty loud blast, so that night we got to work under the cobweb-raftered cellar of Jimmy and Johnny's melancholy house at the corner of Eighth and Gordon—where it stood under a streetlight—parentless as had become usual. We pried the red tabs out of the brass shells and emptied the powder onto newspaper. For a container we planned to use the aluminum flare casing that we had found on the maneuvers field. It was the size of, well, of an oversized stick of dynamite.

In advance, we had banged a nail hole into the side of the canister to accommodate the little green thirty-second fuses from Martin's variety store. Norman held the canister on its end and we poured the gunpowder in using a funnel made of the newspaper. It filled to about three-quarters. The problem then was: how do we seal the end of the canister? Before the rest of us could register a protest, crazy Norman had started banging the end closed against the cement wall of the cellar by using a hammer. The rest of us had scattered and rolled onto the floor and under the workbenches like dust kittens, cradling our heads in our arms and assuming fetal positions, for: if a spark hit the powder ***it would have blown that little house into toothpicks***. But that is not what happened. Instead, he had expertly closed it like a toothpaste tube. We grabbed our big firecracker, matches, fuses, flashlights, and headed for the dump.

❧

The public entrance to the dump was on Mechanic Street where the refuse of Leominster's good citizens was pushed off of the valley wall created by the Nashua. We, however, approached it from bottom, passing through the baseball field off of Twelfth Street down into the valley by the filter beds and up the fire road to the foot of the trash heap which loomed as a cliff 80 feet above us—that night just a black silhouette. To make it easier to light the explosive, we pulled a discarded stuffed chair from the rubbish to use as a launching pad and proceeded.

Norman inserted the 30-second fuse, lit it, and we all ran like hell...but the fuse burned out and nothing happened. "Dud," Johnny had yelled which got a laugh. Norman repeated the process several times with the rest of us watching. Every time, Johnny yelled "Dud," and we all ran but each time not as far as the time before. We were fast losing faith that it would go off at all. Eventually though the fuses caught the chair on fire and it began to burn robustly, illuminating the dump wall, the clearing and us. We had become contentedly mesmerized by the burning chair on which the fire now revealed a cheery floral print fabric that must have been the pride of someone's living room back in some happier time.

Suddenly the canister ignited—but not like dynamite as we had expected—but rather like a whirligig slowly spinning up with a rooster tail of flame and sparks shooting from the fuse hole—a roaring Phoenix rising. It made an abrupt turn then headed for us at waist height and we wheeled and ran for our lives.

Freeze-frame: picture four teenage boys running single-file, through an illuminated clearing in the woods. All are looking back in horror at the flaming monster that is chasing them. Their backs are arched as if to buy an extra inch of protection and they look like cartoon characters. If the picture had a caption it would be: *"Feets don't fail me now."*

⅋

*Coda:*

*Unfreeze-frame: just as it was about to hit the last running boy (me), it veered off and made an abrupt turn straight up and rocketed into the starry sky where it spent its fuel and disappeared to sputter out in the blackness.*

*Davy, Davy Crockett*

# EAST SIDE LOOP

*Prelude:*
*I think that today I will not reminisce about rolling over in cars, nearly being blown to bits, stuck in a cave or beaten by the police. Nothing supernatural will happen. Neither will there be any UFOs, little green men or Sasquatch. This is just a snapshot of the Plastic City from the 1950s, times which—contrary to popular belief—were in living color, not black and white.*

☙

**Picture if you will a boy** of perhaps seven or eight. He's sitting by himself on the cement front steps of his house at 172 Ninth Street, Leominster, Massachusetts. The same summer sun that has browned his skin has bleached his bang-cut blonde hair to platinum. He is wearing a Red Sox players' shirt, cuffed dungarees, black high-top sneakers and a baseball hat with the brim snapped up as he had seen one worn in an old movie. The fact of the matter is that he feels like a character in a movie.

Ninth Street is the bottom of the F&L (Fitchburg and Leominster) Bus Company's East Side Loop which encompasses French Hill. One of its buses rattles by with no passengers at the windows. From here it will make its way back downtown via Water Street. Once the bus is gone it grows quiet once more, almost silent in fact, save for the voice of Arthur Godfrey intoning something like, "huwoya, huwoya huwoya," emanating through the screen door behind him and the cicadas humming metallically from the vacant lot diagonally across the street.

Suddenly, to his delight, his first friend, Wayne, rides by on a huge black dog. He is hanging onto its collar with one hand while holding the other up in the air like a rodeo cowboy. Wayne is so busy with his stunt that he doesn't acknowledge the boy as he rides by. He and his mount turn onto Vezina Avenue and disappear from view.

The boy is now thirsty and asks his mother for money for a Coca-Cola. Cote's Junkyard is at the end of Ninth Street and they have a machine. He walks up the street. The sun has made the new tar hot and soft under his feet and it sticks to his sneakers with each footstep despite the light coat of sand that reminds him of confectioners' sugar. It smells delicious though, as does the heated straw in the humming vacant lot.

When he gets to Cote's he enters the garage, goes to the Coke machine and deposits his dime. It is an old manual device and he can't get the big handle to revolve the Coke bottles over to the dispenser. Reluctantly he asks a mechanic to help him with the machine. The mechanic is lying on a creeper underneath a car but he is good enough to break into his repair work to help the kid out. His face is sweating from his labor in the heat but he does the good deed and even rewards himself with one. The boy takes a sip of the syrupy Coke from the frosty, green-tinged bottle as he leaves the garage to walk back down Ninth. Once again he sits down on his front steps to finish the tonic and resume his vigil. An hour later the F&L bus goes by again.

⚘

**Wayne**

As I wrote this an oil rig burned in the Gulf of Mexico. This made me think again of Wayne. I guess you could say he was my first friend. I was so young that I don't remember meeting him for the first time. His family lived on Tenth Street a block away from mine. When my mother and father bought and moved into our house on Ninth, Wayne and his little sister Susan were the first ones to knock on our door, curious to know if there were any new children in the neighborhood that they could play with. There was, but he was still a baby and they would have to wait a while, my mother had told them. She *did* let them know that my name was Johnny. At regular intervals they would show up and ask if Johnny could come out and play yet. She would tell them, "not yet," until, eventually, I was.

Wayne was something of a comic and he reminded me of Donald O'Connor. He was always trying to act grown up and I noticed that he used a lot of the same expressions of speech that his father used. He loved dogs and went through two of them while I knew him—Rex and King.

In time the circle of friends in the neighborhood grew and Wayne became another one of the larger group. I can remember watching Elvis Presley on his family's black and white television set. Elvis performed on the *Tommy Dorsey Show* for several weeks in a row and by the end of that summer it seemed like everybody was talking about him. Once "Hound Dog" hit the airwaves, I was hooked. I was walking around everyday just singing "Hound dog, hound dog," over and over.

Wayne grew up and went his own way. I ran into him once in Rockdale's discount store years later while looking around at stuff with my then girlfriend. He was in the Navy home on leave and was wearing the white swabby uniform. When I asked him what he had been up to he spoke of "shoveling shit against the tide" which sounded like something his father would say. I could see that my girlfriend was impressed by him

55

though which made me uneasy. I was not even in his league.

℘

*Coda:*

> *Years later my mother read in the Leominster Enterprise that Wayne had been killed. The article stated that he had been working on an oil rig in a place as strange as Brazoria, Texas, on the Gulf of Mexico when an explosion and fire took his life at 26. My mother, who by this time was virtually housebound by panic attacks, was very impressed by the glamorous sound of the job and its exotic locale.*

*Ninth Street, 1972*

# KILROY WAS THERE

*Prelude:*
*Someone once said that there are no haunted houses; only haunted people. I'm inclined to agree.*

**In 1971 I had moved** in with my girlfriend Susan. We rented a second floor apartment in a two-family house on Haverhill Street in Dracut off of Route 110, not far from her parents' house in neighboring Lowell. Susan and I had met at a nightclub called the Three Copper Men where my band, the Katzenjammer Kids, had been performing all of that previous winter.

Strange things soon began happening in that apartment. In one episode, she had been in the bedroom watching television with the lights off while I was taking a shower. The lights had been on in the kitchen and the hall and a silhouette appeared in the doorway, bent over peeking into the bedroom, sort of like the "Kilroy Was Here" cartoon from the WWII years—but sideways.

"Quit trying to scare me," she had said to it, thinking it was me. "I mean it," she said, "You're scaring me."

When I did finally come out of the shower she laid into me for what she thought I'd done. She did not appreciate people trying to freak her out. I explained to her that I hadn't done a thing. She seemed not to believe me but the incident passed and was forgotten. We had no idea what had happened.

A short while later, I awakened from my sleep and sat up. Something was wrong in the room. I turned to my right and there to the other side of Susan was a teenaged boy. I could see him clearly in bluish glow of the streetlight that was right outside of our bedroom window, sitting up, just like I was, looking back at me. He was shirtless and had a medium build and dirty blond hair that was growing out of a short-clip haircut. He looked at me sadly. The commotion woke Susan and as she sat up, the spectre faded and vanished. I began to explain to her what I had seen.

After I had described him to her she said, "That sounds like Tooky Dekker." Tooky had been a high school friend of hers who once had a crush on her, or so she told me. He had been involved in an automobile accident that had taken his young life. This was the first death of a friend for most of the kids at Lowell High School and the wake was hugely attended. When Susan took her turn on the kneeler to pray over Tooky's casket, she noticed that there was dirt under his fingernails. This macabre detail had stayed with her ever since.

*Coda:*

*We moved to the Plastic City soon after these events. The decision to relocate was not connected to the haunting but rather strictly financial—as in—we had no jobs and no money. The apartment on the second floor of my mother's house was available and I knew that the rent would be (very) manageable.*

*Not long after having settled in, there was another late night, another moonlit room and another visitation. Tooky was there again on the opposite side of the bed staring at me in that same way. This time I threw my right fist at his face and of course, the punch contacted nothing. Tooky just looked sad again and slowly vanished—this time for good.*

*Geno and I suited-up for church*

# MASS

**I was raised as a Catholic**, which is to say my parents were
Catholics, and so although I went to public school, I attended
Catechism once a week, made my First Communion and had
been confirmed as one. My parents were not churchgoers and
neither was I. When the guilt began to gnaw at me enough
though, I would make the effort to go to Sunday Mass. For a
while Geno came with me. He'd meet me at my house and we
would walk the six blocks to St. Cecelia's. There was a coffee
shop across the street from the church called Roy's Luncheonette
and oh how it beckoned when we would pass it by. It would
have been so easy to turn left instead of right and have a cup of
coffee, a chocolate-covered donut and some jukebox music. We
called the owner Father Roy which was made funnier by the
fact that there actually was a priest at the church by that name.

We always managed to be late and ended up standing in
the vestibule and peeking through the doors into the nave. A

young priest got wise to us and started coming back there to try to get us to sit down. This one Sunday he succeeded and perp-walked us down to the front, six pews away from the pulpit.

Now, in these times, the church was packed, and everyone, including the stern Monsignor, giving his sermon in French, gawked at us as we were hauled down the aisle. We were wearing our church-going black suits with skinny black ties and cheap, pointy Italian shoes that we'd bought at Rockdale's. Awkwardly we made our way to the center of the pew, excusing ourselves while tripping over the kneelers and stepping on feet—sounds echoing off of the granite and marble in the cavernous nave.

Once we were settled, the Monsignor resumed his sermon. Now, at this point, I should add that this was pre-Vatican 2 Catholicism and also that this French-Canadian congregation did not take the practice of their belief lightly. It was serious business.

The sun was flooding down through the amber-stained windows of the steeple, spotlighting us in gold. You could have heard a pin drop, save for the booming baritone voice of the Monsignor and people clearing their throats and rustling paper. I could not bring myself to look at the priest and I desperately wanted this part of the Mass to be over because I knew that once he finished the *Homily*, he would go back to the altar, finish the ritual in indecipherable Latin and then free us.

In this state of emergency, my senses became heightened and, as time slowed down, I became acutely aware of my surroundings. The statues of Mary, Jesus and Saint Francis seemed to judge us as did the bas-relief figures on the Stations-of-the-Cross. A blue-haired lady sitting in front of me was wearing a stole composed of a string of minks, each one biting the tail of the one in front of it, thus forming a chain. Their little mouths bit like clothes pins on the tails of the ones in front and there were even tiny eyes above their snouts, enhancing the realism. One of the little weasels actually seemed to be looking at me.

All of this began to strike me as enormously funny and a laugh impulse began to take hold of me. I panicked and tried to suppress it, but at that moment, I made the fatal error: *I looked at Geno.*

And lo, the floodgates dideth burst. The laugh that Geno had been stifling in his own belly would no longer be denied and up it came, rising in volume and in pitch as it did so. The Monsignor now paused again. His face reddened and his eyes began to bulge from their sockets. His red neck strained against his collar. Now totally at the mercy of his laughing jag, Geno did the only thing that made any sense; he got up and stumbled across the pew again, excusing himself in-between peals of laughter, knocking over prayer books and mimeographed copies as he went. He did, however, have the presence-of-mind to turn toward the altar and genuflect as he'd been taught, but then wheeled and hustled up the aisle, his head thrown back on his muscular neck, hooting like a screech monkey under a full moon. He plowed through the heavy swinging doors and was free.

I, on the other hand, was not so lucky. I was the accomplice, the whole congregation knew it, and I sensed the hundreds of black French eyes focused on the duck's-ass back of my haircut. That Mass seemed to last for several hours more but eventually it did in fact come mercifully to an end.

⨏

*Coda:*

*The following Sunday we went to Mass again. We were late as usual, so we were peeking through the doors at the service. The same young priest appeared but this time he told us that if we weren't going to go in and sit down we should leave and not come back. From then on we started going for coffee, donuts and jukebox music at Roy's on Sunday mornings; taking the left, not the right. We assuaged our guilt with the knowledge that we could at least see the closed doors (a huis clos) of the church through the plate glass window of the luncheonette just across Mechanic Street as the Mass was being celebrated.*

63

*Left to right: Edward, Irene, Peggy, John and Helen*

# THE DIVIL YE KNOW

**Growing up we had a dog** named Waggy. She was a Chow mix, 17-years-old and half blind. Wags had been my mother's family's dog but with my grandmother now getting on in years and alone in her house, care of the pet had become burdensome, so my mother volunteered to take her off of Nana's hands. This was not a boy-and-his-dog situation. She was a lot older than I was and had pretty much seen it all in her time with my mother's big family. The dog was understandably burned-out, and I learned to expect little enthusiasm from her and not be disappointed. She seemed to view my childish vigor with a look of apprehension. Nonetheless we did love the old girl.

&

**Pete**

In the Gallagher home, Wags had been the successor to a pooch name Pete. Pete had been a star in the family—one of the great pets of which—like the great women—you only get so many in life. My grandfather had gotten him as a puppy.

The family that Pete shepherded grew large. There was handsome fledgling actor, **John** (my namesake) who died in a car accident at 21 (the cops came in the middle of the night to inform the parents and God knows how hard Nana took it as she was distraught at the slightest injury to her children).

**Irene** came next in birth order. She was so pretty that a wealthy Fitchburg family proposed adopting her because Hugh and Hannah had so many other mouths to feed. The offer was not accepted.

**Edward** worked in the Civilian Conservation Corps to help with family finances and later joined the Navy, escorting supply ships in the North Atlantic during WWII. After the war he worked for Grandpa's employer: Crocker Paper.

**Hubert Jr. (Bat)** came next but was institutionalized with a horrible childhood illness which paralyzed him for the full 21 years of his life.

**Helen** (my mother) was another beauty in the family, known for her good taste in clothes and the soft heart that would always be a there with a little money if one of the siblings fell short.

Then there was **Peggy** whom the kids called "The Queen" because of her sassy ways. Family legend has it that she threw a radio at Grandpa because he had turned it off while she was listening to it, supposedly because they had company. Peggy wasn't intimidated by my sometimes irascible grandfather's bluster and would actually confront him about things unlike everyone else. You know he loved her for that.

A child named **Mary** was born next but she expired very young and was not spoken of at any length in the family as was the custom in those days.

Next came **Ray**, a larger-than-life personality and a handsome scrapper with a million-dollar smile and a great left hook. He sought his fortune on the West Coast.

Next came lovely sweet-tempered **Teresa** followed by **Paul**, who died in infancy.

**Bobby** was the baby. Especially considering his humble origins, he has led an astonishingly accomplished life as an educator and psychologist, but in youth, he was not adverse to picking up a couple of nickels by escorting his friends up to the barn loft which had a commanding view of the bathroom window through which his older sisters could be spied upon as they sponge-bathed.

&

**Nana** (Hannah) had immigrated at 19 from Knochmanagh, Kilarney, County Kerry in Ireland, sponsored by the McGowans; Margaret (Aunt Mag) and John. She found work as a maid and cook for wealthy Fitchburg households until meeting and marrying **Grandpa** (Hugh), moving into the big company-owned house next to the mill in West Fitchburg and starting their family. Grandpa was a Roman Catholic from Protestant Belfast in Northern Ireland. He had landed a job at Crocker Paper Company where he developed a reputation for being an outstanding papermaker, so good in fact that the company moved him from that mill to their most prestigious one to become what they called a "Machine Tender." He was the person who was in charge of a particular high-end paper making machine. He faced animosity from the other employees because he was considered an outsider as well as for his expertise, so it was a hard time for him, something he may have been familiar with from his upbringing in Belfast. Perhaps for this reason, when he was offered a promotion to become boss over all the machines in Number Eight mill, he turned it down.

Grandpa was a responsible father when the early batch of kids were born until he took a part-time job bartending at the British-American Club down near the river to bring in extra money. Over time he became one of the clubs better customers having contracted a certain well-known Irish malady. But he never missed work and always brought home a paycheck, even in the worst of the Depression years. His delicate condition could make him cantankerous though and Nana sometimes suffered the brunt while their brood took cover. When friends asked her why she stayed with him, she always answered in the charming brogue that she never lost, "Better the divil ye know than the divil ye don't know." As to why she continued adding mouths to feed during those lean years: in her patented dry delivery, she always answered, "Well, it took me 11 times to get to the bottom of what was causing the pregnancies."

&

In the end Pete had greatly enhanced the lives of the Gallaghers, but this relationship had gotten off to a rocky start. Grandpa, who had brought the mongrel home in the first place, disliked the way it was chewing up everything in the house, and even though the kids now adored the dog, he decided to get rid of him. He gave Pete to a man who lived up in New Hampshire which created a lot of wailing and gnashing of teeth in the household. Two weeks later, the dog showed up on the doorstep. Grandpa said, "If he went to all that trouble to get back, he belongs here."

With that, Pete became a member-in-good-standing of the Gallagher clan. He was always called by name and treated with extreme *politesse*. There was; "God Bless you Pete," when he sneezed and; "Excuse me Pete," when you had to step over him in passing. People in the neighborhood greeted him with a; "Good morning, Mr. Peter Gallagher," when their paths crossed. On Sundays when the family put on the good clothes Nana had made them and marched off to Mass at St. John's, Pete and the other neighborhood dogs followed them up to wait outside. When the bells would peal, all the dogs would howl and the kids had all they could do not to piss themselves to keep from laughing.

*Beyond this portal there be monsters*

# OLD MILL ROAD MONSTER

**One day in the early part** of the 1960s, a kid we knew, a Saxon Trade student named Charlie, went walking in the woods off of Old Mill Road. He was armed with his squirrel gun and was pissing away the morning scouting out targets of opportunity. At the edge of a small clearing he saw—on the far side—some creature staring back at him, nearly hidden by the foliage. It was taller than he, at least six-feet-tall and maybe more. At first he thought it might be a bear and prepared to make a run for it, but there was also something human about it that lessened his apprehension and his curiosity won out.

He cautiously walked step-by-step across the clearing towards this entity. It didn't move, but merely stood its ground and regarded him evenly. Charlie could now see that it was more like an ape than a bear, but it was not like any one he had ever seen or heard of before. He was only a few yards from it when it lunged forward and grabbed him by the arm but he was able to break free and run for his life.

Charlie told some friends about the encounter, exhibiting the scratches and welts on his arm as proof. The story spread through the Plastic City like wildfire.

⅋

Stories about "Bigfoot" in the Pacific Northwest had been around since the early-1800s, but they did not get a lot play in the media until 1967 when there surfaced widely-circulated film footage of what was purportedly one such creature shambling across a clearing in Bluff Creek, California. In the early 1960s though, very few people had heard of Bigfoot where I come from. Connoisseur of the *outré* that I fancied myself to be would certainly have read something of it but I had not. And it is doubtful to me that Charlie would have either—but read on and decide on your own.

⅋

Having been weaned on monster movies at the Metropolitan and Plymouth theaters, we, the teenagers of Leominster, knew that we had to mobilize to investigate the situation and mobilize we did. Those who did not have cars jumped into the cars of those who did, and a ragtag motorcade converged onto spooky, remote Old Mill Road. The Saturday night *TAG* dance at City Hall would have to wait until the following week—this week we had work to do.

There were no houses on that lonely stretch of road and it was something of a Lovers' Lane on most weekends but not on this one. A fleet of 1950s and 1960s cars barreled up the road, radios blaring, bodies hanging out of windows, banging fists on the doors and whistling through their fingers. But once you crossed under the ancient stone railroad underpass, the mood became more somber. You were now in the Monster's world.

The cars pulled over and onto the soft shoulders at odd angles parking wherever they could find room and the kids jumped out. The classic cars (to be) were left running and the headlights shone up into the woods casting weird shadows.

70

WEIM blared from the open windows as we invaded the woods casting long shadows of our own. I remember seeing a footprint supposedly made by The Monster but it was not terribly conclusive as evidence.

We kept at it though—Lunchies and Packrats alike—all engaged in the same quest, sticking to our cliques but together nonetheless, something that was not the norm, united against a common foe. At one point a mob of kids emerged from the trees shouting, "We got it," and carrying one of their buddies over their shoulders like pallbearers. All-in-all it was a riot-in-the-woods and sweet slice of teenage heaven.

By the next weekend The Monster was still being talked about but although there was *some* activity out on Old Mill Road, by-and-large, interest had waned and everyone went back to doing what they would normally do on Saturday nights which was to go to TAG, get a hot dog from Mike's cart (marvelling at his crazy hand-jive) and driving from one end of downtown to the other, over...and...over...again.

⚘

*Coda:*

*A year or more later, I was sitting in Charlie's Diner downtown at the corner of Mechanic and Main streets nursing a tepid coffee. It was a late Saturday afternoon in Monument Square and a melancholy sun lit the streaked plate glass windows when in walked Charlie the "Monster Man" (no relation to Charlie the restaurant owner). We exchanged handshakes and pleasantries after having not crossed paths in "a dog's age." At some point in the conversation, I couldn't help but ask him about the Old Road Monster incident—his claim to fame. It had always fascinated me and here was the "horse's mouth" so to speak.*

*With "Wolverton Mountain" playing on the jukebox as a sound track, Charlie gave me the straight scoop: it was a hoax after all. He had in fact made the whole thing up as a lark, never expecting things to get as far out-of-hand as they had. His claim to fame had become an albatross around his neck as he'd been hounded with questions ever since. In desperation he had to disavow the story to get everybody off his back.*

*I'd be lying if I said I wasn't disappointed. Maybe it's just a way to print the legend instead of the fact if the legend is better, but I can't help but think that he might have wanted to recant his tale whether true or false. I still can't help but wonder after all these years.*

*"Time Won't Let Me"*

# I WAS A TEENAGE CAVEMAN

**Not long ago**, my wife Jocelyn and I took a drive down to
Worcester (Wistah) from our home in Gloucester (Glostah)
for a change of scenery and to get a shot of culture (culcha).
She'd been reading about the Worcester Art Museum and there
seemed to be enough there to see to make it worthwhile so we
made the trip. Growing up in the Plastic City, Worcester was
the nearest metropolis and I had gone there enough times that
I believed I had a feel for the place. As a child in the Fifties, I
had even seen much of it reduced to piles of rubble that were
once homes in the wake of the Worcester Tornado. By the mid-
Sixties it was a cool destination with its Carnaby Street-style
clothes stores and head shops, all catering to the college crowd,
musicians and hippies.

❧

Worcester had changed since the last time I had seen it.
The neighborhoods looked downtrodden as we drove through

them. The most notable architectural feature of downtown had been City Hall which once had a beautiful, expansive park laid out of it like a front lawn filled with monuments and fountains. This was the orientation site where one could get one's bearings. But no more—City Hall was still there but where the park once was now stands a depressing black slab of architectural dreck.

We made our way up to the museum. It is in an area which must have been intentionally laid out to gather the institutions of learning, culture and government into one spot. All of these grand buildings now seemed huddled together, as if trembling in fear of the shining eyes just outside of the campfire's glow.

After we had immersed ourselves in the museum's collection for the morning, we thought that we would walk down to the commercial area and try to find lunch. As we strolled along, we became impressed by the *façade* of a particularly imposing edifice which turned out to be the Worcester Memorial Auditorium. As we stood on the sidewalk in front of it, I realized that I had some history with the building.

I began to relate to Jocelyn that I had seen the Beach Boys there when it was comprised of the brothers Brian, Carl and Dennis Wilson along with Mike Love and Al Jardine. They had sounded great, but I did notice that the brothers all looked pretty well-fed and would probably be looking at larger sizes of white pants and striped shirts for their next tour. I'd also seen the Byrds there, one of my favorite groups to this day. And then I remembered that I too had played there many moons before.

&

The year was 1966 and the Cavemen had been hired to be the featured act at a battle-of-the-bands being held at the auditorium. We, however, would not be in the contest— we were the professionals (even being paid). Our band was something of a known entity in the area having played regularly at a popular dance at neighboring Leicester airport.

The set-up was that we would do three short sets—opening

the show, a middle slot and then closing. The contestant bands would play in between.

And that's the way it went. All of these young musicians had lots of friends and the big hall was packed. Even though band uniforms were on the way out of style by this time, the Cavemen looked pretty sharp that night. Our signature outfit was the leopard skin, Beatles-cut jacket worn with a white shirt, black tie, black pants and Verde "Beatle boots." Outfit two was the same except that the jackets were black with some leopard skin on the collars and pockets. The latest duds reflected the changing times and they were dark red microsuede pullover shirts with rawhide laces at the throat also with leopard skin at the collar and white jeans. Each time we came out, we'd changed into something different and it was pretty slick I guess.

At one point during the show, I was singing "Time Won't Let Me" and I heard a female voice yelling, "Hey...hey you," from the balcony which gracefully flared out near the stage in effect forming box seats. I looked up in curiosity and the whole section, all girls, erupted in screams. It had finally happened—I'd had my *"Beatle Moment!"*

&#x25ac;&#x36;

After we had finished our closing set and the crowd was filing out, about 12 or perhaps as many as 20 kids came over to the stage to see me. Some wanted an autograph but most just wanted to shake hands. I squatted down, flattered, my Gretsch Tennessean still dangling from my shoulder, my left hand steadying the guitar at the neck. Now: one of the occupational hazards playing rock and roll is the possibility of electrical shock. I myself had been knocked onto my back and unconscious from the zap of a microphone.

As it happened on this night, a low level of current was passing from the outlet, to the amp, up the cord to my guitar, from the guitar up my arm and then through my hand into the hands that I was shaking. The kids were all reacting, literally in shock. They walked away cradling their right hands in their

75

lefts. One guy mock-staggered off crying for all the world to hear, "He's electric, HE'S ELECTRIC!"

*Before the Packrats (circa 1963)...there were Cats*

# THE CATS

**As I have stated previously,** on French Hill in the Fifties, we walked into the woods and vanished into the trees much like those ghostly baseball players in the movie *Field of Dreams*. Some of us had rules that required us home by the time the street lights went on. For others, myself included, it was something more nebulous, like, in time for supper. We were not chauffeured. We walked to school, to the corner stores and to the movies. But in the summer, and on weekends; it was the woods beyond Twelfth Street that beckoned us.

At Twelfth we stepped into our own field of dreams, the field itself, the side of the Nashua valley wall, the Little Nashway, the filter beds, the fire road that led up to the foot of the wall of refuse that was the city dump and then the Nashua proper. In this place we divided into rival teams and fought our mock wars with toy guns. We shot frogs, birds and rats at the dump with our BB guns (guilty memories). The rats were too tough to kill with BBs and once hit would just wheel around and go in a different direction, just like targets in the shooting games at Whalom Park (ding, ding, ding).

We had our own portal into our stomping grounds. It was marked by a tree at the crest of the incline down to the floodplain. For a while there was a "Tarzan" swing tied to a branch on the tree, but that lasted only long enough to cause a few injuries and soon just a nub of the rope remained. This tree served as our assembly point when we were being chased either by the police or an indignant home owner who had taken issue with the fact that we had stolen from his apple orchard or tomato garden. "Meet at the tree," someone would shout as we scattered and meet we would, winded and laughing.

Where there are now two Little League fields there was once only one. I remember resenting the construction of the first diamond and outfield as encroachment of our territory, but we used it for a some pickup baseball of our own, splitting into teams. One time Jimmy drove around the bases repeatedly in his father's car with me riding shotgun when we were about 13 (a story for another time). In the Fifties though it was just a semi-clearing on the plateau with a sandbank on one side that ran down to Mechanic Street.

&

For me, growing up, there were only two things to fear for a kid: bigger kids and global thermonuclear war. Adults seemed benign and oblivious to us, so it was unnerving when one day, years before the Little League fields, a hand-built hobo shack appeared in the clearing. I was told in hushed tones that it had been built there by the "Cats," mysterious creatures who were neither kids nor adults but were to be feared. Nobody seemed to know who they were and we never saw them, but the shack was physical proof of their existence.

It follows that the Cats' girlfriends were called "Kittens" and I was informed that certain Kittens were known to cut off the tips of their brassieres so that their *mammillae* would show through their fuzzy angora sweaters—a detail I found completely bewildering at the time. It was an uncomfortable feeling to think that some malevolent force was haunting these woods that we thought we knew so well. The woods we thought we owned.

The day we first saw it we stopped in our tracks and stared at it. It was just too provocative to ignore, like the black monolith in *Space Odyssey 2001*. We inched over towards it nervous in our bellies, prepared to bolt. Claude tiptoed over first and boldly pushed aside the blanket that served as a door in the opening and peeked in. They were not there, so we all went in, halfway expecting angry Cats to show up at any minute to... kill us? There wasn't much in there; some furniture from the dump; beer cans, bottle caps, cigarette butts and an out-of-date cheesecake garage calendar hanging on the wall.

Andy picked up a small object and held it up for us to see. It was a little top hat expertly crafted from beer cans, a visor and a crown: *prison art*. What resonates to this day is the fact that it would be a perfect fit for a real cat. Some Cat had killed a little time in the hobo shack drinking beer, checking out the calendar, smoking and making that little hat.

🐾

*Coda:*

*We walked past the Cats' shack for weeks after that first encounter, never seeing a sign of occupancy. In time, we lost our fear of the place and began to destroy it, little-by-little. We jumped on the roof, smashed the windows that were not already smashed and knocked down the walls. We never saw the Cats and in time all evidence of the hobo shack dissolved into the earth and the woods returned to us.*

*My best Elvis*

# TELSTAR

*Prelude:*
  *Let it be said up front: I love animals, pretty much all of them. I would never intentionally hurt one and have nearly flipped my car avoiding a chipmunk on the road. I try not to step on ants and take bees and spiders outside using the glass-and-paper method to set them free. But sometimes, events can make one behave out-of -character, and my experience with Telstar—with apologies—was one such time.*

**Kids of my generation** were brought up on cowboy shows. In the Fifties the television programs were aimed at us, and our heroes were Hopalong Cassidy, The Cisco Kid, The Lone Ranger, Gene Autry, Roy Rogers, Matt Dillon and on and on. Zorro and Davy Crockett might even fit in as sub-genres. Ushering in the Sixties were *Sugarfoot, Maverick, Bronco, The Rebel (great theme song), Have Gun Will Travel, Cheyenne,*

*Wagon Train, Death Valley Days, Wyatt Earp, Bat Masterson, The Rifleman* and more. At the movies, all of the major stars eventually mounted horses and put on signature hats. They portrayed men of action and honor. Good with their guns, their fists and to their word. And everybody got to wear the same clothes everyday. How could you beat that?

All of which brings us inevitably to the horse. Every cowboy has to have one. We, of course, could not in our compact suburb-of-nothing neighborhood. Monetary and logistical factors aside, horse ownership was just not practical. A rabbit or a rooster maybe. Oh you might have a friend of a friend who had horses, but if you didn't, you rented a steed at one of the handful of stables in the area to ride out your cowboy fantasies—so to speak. It was on one such outing that I encountered Telstar.

&

A bunch of us went out to a somewhat low-rent stable and acquired a half-dozen mounts and headed out for their trail late one Sunday afternoon. The one I got was named Telstar. Telstar had one eye that had been blinded from an incident on that same trail—or so I was told up front. Anyway; I had drawn poor bottom-of-the-barrel Telstar and accepted my lot with cowboy stoicism. Our party trotted off down a path through the woods led by a guide. At one point Telstar stopped cold for no apparent reason. He wouldn't budge. The guide tried to coax the horse around the spot to no avail.

At this point I began to grow embarrassed, especially in front of the girls, feeling like the greenhorn from *Back East* who can't get his nag to move. The sun was getting low and I was holding up the party. "You guys go ahead, I'll catch up to you," I said waving them off. With faces full of concern they turned their horses and rode off toward the setting sun. Our guide gave me one last unconvinced look then wheeled around to attend to the other riders.

Now it was just Telstar and me in the gathering gloom.

With the others gone, it grew very quiet, the only sounds being the buzzing and chirping of night bugs and birds along with Telstar's robust breathing. I tried riding and then leading him to every alternative path to get by that spot but the horse was having none of it. Time was passing and it was becoming darker. Eventually, my increasing aggravation got the better of me. I dismounted still holding onto the reins and stepped over to the side of the horse's head that had the good eye so that he could see me. First I apologized and then punched him on the side of his head. Telstar's eye grew wide—white showing all around the iris—then he bolted. I jumped back onto the saddle like a Sioux warrior and we took off.

Telstar chose his own route around the trouble spot and back onto the main trail, stopping along the way to try to scrape me off against a large tree like I was shit on a boot. I wriggled over to the other side and clung to the saddle like a circus monkey.

Horse and rider now broke free of the wooded trail and headed up the outer edge of a small horseshoe canyon (which was actually an excavation site). Telstar was at a full gallop. I eased back onto the western saddle and regained my posture— reins in my right hand—left arm akimbo. My hair blew back from my face, the sun turned the clouds blood red and the cowboy orchestra in my mind piped up the theme from *The Magnificent Seven* or the Marlboro Man if you prefer.

Telstar and I barrel-assed up one side of the canyon rim and down the other, then finally along the last leg of the trail to the barn where my friends were waiting and the guide was preparing to go back looking for us.

When we galloped into the paddock, the horse stopped on a dime throwing clods of earth into the air. I swung my right leg over the saddle horn and jumped off with the ease of a Pony Express rider spiking my landing. In all modesty, I would have to confess that it was one of my better entrances.

*Flat-top Cat*

# LADY OF SPAIN

**Elvis Presley seemed to be** everywhere in the summer of 1956.
I first saw him for several consecutive weeks on *The Dorsey
Brothers Stage Show* which was replacing Jackie Gleason during
his seasonal hiatus. Presley came on doing cover versions from
his stage set; stuff like Big Joe Turner's "Shake Rattle and Roll"
and Little Richard's "Tutti-Frutti." But Elvis was making them
all his own in woozy black and white images on America's
bulky television consoles.

The live studio audiences reacted with shrieks and nervous
giggles, applauding after he bumped and grinded during
Scotty Moore's guitar solos as if the young singer with the
sideburns had just done a dance routine. Once he hit with his
own "Heartbreak Hotel," he just seemed to expand to fill the
universe. Appearances with Milton Berle, Steve Allen and Ed
Sullivan followed in quick succession over the next year and a
half and I was totally hooked.

So it followed that Elvis became my idol—and one emulates one's idol, doesn't one? Work commenced on my *pompadour*. The first weapons of choice were a tube of Brylcreem (a little dab'l do ya) and a Plastic City comb. My shirts were now worn with the collars turned up. The sideburns would have to wait until I grew up a little. My mirror might reflect me practicing my crooked smile or my Elvis moves, using a tennis racket as a guitar—lip-synching to my handful of 45 rpm records.

However to take it to the next level, I knew that I would need a *real* guitar. So I asked my mother if I could take guitar lessons. She suggested that I take the more conventional accordion instead, reasoning that if I could learn to play one instrument, another would be easier to learn. Plus there was a teacher right in the neighborhood. This was not what I had in mind, but I took it as a distasteful bump along the path to my own personal *"Elvisness."*

⚘

And that was how I found myself on the sunporch of a gentleman who taught accordion to supplement his income at the corner of Eighth and Mechanic streets, one block from my house. The previous week he had taken me through the fundamentals of the instrument and sent me home to practice "Hot Cross Buns" as a homework assignment. On the second Saturday he measured my progress (not much) and gave me some more pointers. He had a huge gorgeous red accordion with ornate inlays and it all looked very expensive—in sharp contrast to my little grey mother-of-pearl student unit rented from Metro Music Mart. He might have sensed that I was quickly losing what little enthusiasm that I had and that may be why he invited his son, Randy, to sit in on my lesson.

Randy was a year ahead of me in school and was working on an Elvis conk of his own. The goop in his hair was making *his* face break out in pimples too. He strapped on a nice big accordion (just not as big or as nice as his father's) and undid the latches that held the bellows shut. The accordion inhaled a little on its own as if it were catching its breath. Father and son conferred for a second then nodded in unison. On a three-count they launched into "Lady of Spain," a wildly popular hit in its day—and *the* accordion song.

The sunporch exploded with music. They smiled affectionately at one another as they played the song's melody and harmony on their gleaming instruments. Notes were whirling and twirling. I sat with my little rental idle on my lap and watched in slack-jawed awe as their ring-bejeweled fingers danced and pranced expertly up and down the black and white keys on the right side while their fingers danced a *Tarantella* across the bass buttons on the left (oompah oompah oompah). Each verse upped the ante from the verse before—more tricks, more notes. The bellows rose and fell like the lungs of a marathon runners. I halfway expected the mother to come dancing in from the kitchen playing the Castanets with a rose clenched in her teeth.

The song ended with a crescendo of notes and a *cha-cha-cha*. When they looked at me for my reaction I may have been able to manage a "wow" but they were so in-the-zone I doubt that they would have even noticed. Like spent lovers they were, speechless and winded. With my time now up, and with the next budding Myron Floren slumped forlornly on the settee in the front hall, my teacher gave me another assignment and said he would see me the following week. I latched my little squeezebox's bellows closed and interred it into its imitation alligator case for what I knew would be the last time. I gave him my three dollars and said that yes, I would see him on Saturday. But that was a lie. What my mind said was; "this is futile…I will never do that…good-bye," and I bounded home to give my mother the bad/good news.

&

*Coda:*

*So what lesson had I learned from "Lady of Spain?" I had learned that next time I was going to hold out for a guitar. Rock and roll singers don't play accordions for crying out loud!*

*Dom Tata (right), Miami, 1945*

# A SLEEPING PROPHET

*Prelude:*

*I'm sleeping but my eyes are darting back and forth under my eyelids. In what had been the grey/black death of unconsciousness flickering images have appeared. Like something from an old movie, a steam train billowing smoke from its stack is barreling down a track right to left. The scene shifts to a second mirror image train racing in from the left. Back to the right, then to the left with increasing speed. They are on the same track and it is painfully clear what is about to happen. But although they still race towards their destinies, they have changed natures and are now automobiles. The scenes shift more quickly now—left and then right—until the shattering inevitable happens.*

⅋

**Upon the impact I sit up** in bed and scream—now wide-awake. It is enough of a disturbance to awaken my mother who comes to my red-painted room concerned. I tell her about the dream but the details dissolve upon telling. After a while I fall back to sleep and thankfully dream no more that night.

## Tamor Plastics

In the early-Sixties, my father Anthony Tata and his brother Domenic were making plans to move their company's operations to Lawrence, Massachusetts for business reasons. For me this constituted a personal disaster. The friends that you have at 14 are at the forefront of your life. I didn't look forward to leaving them, my home or the Plastic City, but by the way it was going, we would be pulling up stakes...and soon. I so hated the idea that I lay in bed before sleep every night and prayed that something would happen to change this course of affairs.

## Domenic

Dom had done well with his share of the company profits. He owned a redwood-sided executive ranch on Route 13 that would not be out of place in Hollywood with its circular driveway and kidney-shaped swimming pool in the back. It was quite a departure from the rest of the expensive but traditional architecture on that side of town—way on the other side of the tracks from French Hill where we lived. There were always at least one and sometimes two Cadillacs in the driveway and at one point they hired a floor boy from the shop to chauffeur them around, costuming him in a grey monkey suit right down to the jodhpurs, boots and a visored cap. I loved pointing out the house to my friends from the window of the F&L bus on the way to Whalom Park.

## The Accident

The night of my dream, Domenic and his party had been returning from an evening out at the Sulkies. The guys were up front with Dom driving the big Caddy with his buddy riding shotgun. The ladies were in the back—my aunt Lucille and the friend's wife. There was a head-on collision with another vehicle and both men were killed. The women survived but were seriously injured. This catastrophe had occurred at the exact moment that I had sat up screaming and was comforted by my mother.

&

## The Aftermath

The morning after the night of my dream as we rustled around the house sleepy-eyed; the phone rang. My mother took the call and then with *gravitas* handed the phone to my father. He listened and asked some questions being rendered ashen by the answers. His brother had died. After he hung up and went into the living room in shock, I reminded my mother about the dream that had woken us both up at the same time as the accident. She looked at me for a brief moment, her eyes focused on mine and she nodded slightly in recognition, but nothing more was said. There were bigger things to consider that morning than dreams.

&

*Coda:*

*The company went into chaos for a while after the accident as the stakeholders regrouped from the loss of their leader. They never did move from the Plastic City and neither did we move from Ninth Street. Over the course of time, Lucille went on to helm the operation then followed by their son, Micky. After that I moved away and lost sight of Tamor's direction. My father had divested himself and was no longer a player in the company's affairs. What I know is that the building still stands on Carter Street. I have to say that to this day I feel a twinge of guilt that I prayed so hard for something to happen to prevent the move.*

91

*The boy who would be King*

# RAISON D'ETRE

**Back at the beginning** of this little journey that I have christened *The Boy from Plastic City*, I stated as part of my *raison d'être* that I was creating the blog in order to sort through some memories and jot them down before I forgot them in a stream-of-consciousness progression. There is no sequence and the stories seem to let me know when they are to be told. This is a departure from what might constitute a proper autobiography, as is the absence of in-depth fact-checking on my part. Admittedly I have not done that. I have some clues about names, times and places from my old photographs and—with luck—what is notated on their flip-sides. That's about the sum of it. The following story illustrates that void. All I know is what I remember and there is no one left that I can ask for more details. Should such details surface I will update the story.

With my Huck Finn raft now nearing the middle of this lake of reminiscence, I find that one of the more interesting aspects of the process has been about the choices that I am forced to make, i.e.; what to leave out, what to keep in. I wonder if any autobiographer tells his whole story. I doubt it. There are living people's feelings to consider and then there are the dead to be respected. There are disappointments, embarrassments, shame, guilt and let's be honest—most of life is just plain too boring to recount. Although my hope is that someone out there will find humor in the essays, be aware that there is tragedy and violence as well. The good, the bad and the ugly.

By this juncture I have learned that the tales will let me know when they are to be told or if they shall be told at all. Thanks for coming this far. Thus forewarned, you are hereby invited to pole along.

*Jimmy and brother Johnny*

# AURORA

**My friend Jimmy lived in** a little Craft-style cottage on the corner of Gordon Avenue and Eighth Street. Back then Eighth ended abruptly because of a large sinkhole that broke it between Gordon and Spruce. Besides being a geographical anomaly of French Hill, it was not good for much except for some adequate sledding in winter. This small house pulsed with the life of the five children in the brood: **Jimmy** was the youngest, then came **Johnny** (the wild card), **Jeannie** (religiously inclined enough to serve a hitch as a nun), **Dicky** (husky and short-tempered) and **Ronnie** (who would later answer his calling to the priesthood). When I first began visiting their house, all of these kids were still living at home, at least tentatively, and were coming and going constantly.

His father was a wiry, no-nonsense carpenter who struck me as a character from an earlier era. He had a dry "let's-pull-one-over-on-the-city-slickers" sense of humor that could really crack his kids up. Maybe it was the twinkle in his eyes, magnified as they were behind his coke-bottle glasses, but he could say something hysterical like: "yes," and the kids would be on the floor in breathless laughter. Try as they may, his expressions were never as funny when they tried to mimic him.

In my first memory of his mother, she is standing at the stove in the center of the kitchen riding herd on her pots and pans. The kitchen is windowless and the darkest part of it is where she is standing. In her shadows, she seems to stare off into some middle-distance, hovering there in her house dress.

In those days you usually summoned a friend out to play by standing outside of the door and calling his name until he showed his face. She came to the side door on one such occasion to inform me through the screen that Jimmy wasn't at home. She spoke as if bemused and it seemed as though the kitchen shadows clung to her even in the brilliant daylight.

She passed away not long after that. Jimmy told me that on the night that she had died, as he was laying in bed crying, the rocking chair that she used to sit on in his room started to move. As it rocked he said he could hear her rhythmic breathing. Naturally I had to ask if there was a window open but he was prepared for any such skepticism and shot that down before the question was fully out of my mouth.

With the passing of the mother, the house became like a rudderless ship. My impression was that the father seemed to distance himself from the house that he had built with his own hands and the children he had helped create. Not that he abandoned them financially—he still provided for them—but he was obviously not going to attempt to fill the void left by their loss and neither would anyone else. In my memory, he seemed to be at home less and less during that period and I got the impression that he was building a new wing onto his life and letting the old part slip into disrepair.

Into this vacuum, brother Dicky appointed himself father surrogate and he would seem to swoop in at the most inopportune times to catch us at whatever he might deem to be an infraction. His justice was swift and merciless on his younger brothers and I was very happy not to be one of them on several occasions.

With the older siblings making new living arrangements, the place got to be like a clubhouse, as under-parented houses tend to do. It was primarily occupied by Johnny, Jimmy and whomever they were chumming around with that day and a lot of times that was me. One of the best games in the empty house was lights out hide-and-seek which was a blast. We also played a lot of cards.

&#8494;

**La Paloma**

In time, Geno joined the crew of this little wooden ship, adrift on its lonely sea. One night after an improvised dinner of *Chef Boyardee* spaghetti, we broke out all 47 of the family's bicycle playing cards (so well marked that they might just as well have been showing their faces) for some penny-ante poker at the kitchen table. At one point, Johnny inexplicably got up from the table and went into his room. He reemerged a minute later with a pump shotgun cradled in his arms.

Now; the sight of a shotgun was not an uncommon one on French Hill, but Johnny, ever the comedian, was making one of his crazy faces. He had a bad tooth in front that added to the dementedness of his expression. We all laughed at him and told him to come back into the game, but when he pumped the gun's action and an unfired shell ejected from the chamber and clattered onto the linoleum floor, we dropped our cards and scattered. He had served notice that this baby was loaded. Johnny stalked his target of choice. It would be a turkey-shoot because he could have caught any of us, but it was me that he cornered against the parlor wall.

I froze as he put the barrel to the side of my head behind my left ear. I rolled my eyes around to see that the same crazed expression was on his face and that his right index finger was

97

twitching on the trigger.

Their brother Ronnie was an audiophile and he had built a beautiful stereo console using mail-order parts from instructions he had found in *Popular Electronics*. We had been listening to my new album, *Don't Knock the Twist* by Chubby Checker while we ate spaghetti and played Poker. In the long, surreal moment that I crouched there with a shotgun to my head, I sadly considered the possibility that the cut that was playing in vivid stereo, "La Paloma Twist," might be the next-to-the-last thing that I would ever hear, although in reality, I probably would not have heard the blast because my skull would have been vacated.

Just then Geno lunged into the parlor and in one continuous motion grabbed the barrel and pushed it up and away from my head, took the shotgun out of Johnny's hands, rested it in a corner, grabbed Johnny, folded him up like a lawn chair and crammed him out of the window (a drop of about four feet).

Once things settled down we all squabbled a little about the incident with Johnny standing outside the window of his own home protesting that it was just a big joke and that we had no sense of humor. As brothers will do, Jimmy dutifully backed him up. We knew we were not going to top that so we broke it up for the night.

Walking down Gordon Avenue I felt blessed to see that the *Aurora Borealis* was active in the northern sky again. It was a rare sight in the Plastic City and it made me feel even more keenly alive, and I whistled "La Paloma Twist" all the way home.

&

*Coda:*

*Playing the game of "What If:" Could the gun have gone off when Geno grabbed it? Quite possibly. Would Johnny have pulled the trigger? Not intentionally. Does Chubby Checker still perform "La Paloma Twist" as part of his stage show? My guess is yes because it might appeal to the Latino demographic.*

*Look to the skies, 1966*

# WHITE SANDS

**After high school I worked** at a Thom McCann shoe warehouse to make some tuition money for art school. The warehouse was near downtown, and it was nice clean work with no heavy lifting—picking orders placed by shoe stores. It sure beat the hell out of operating a broiling molding machine, especially in the heat. All of the rank-and-file employees were only a year or two apart in age and many of us knew each other in passing. It was also a Teamster shop so the pay was halfway decent by Plastic City standards. Demand for shoes was down that summer and between the heat and the lack of orders, activity at the warehouse slowed to a crawl.

There was a cultural shift going on then and my theory is that people were holding off on buying shoes rather than investing in the wrong fashion statement. Our union would protect us from layoffs however so everybody got busy "gettin' busy." Some constructed fragrant reefer dens up in the mountains of shoe cartons while others got good at the new craze of skateboarding on the smooth wooden floors of the second story which was like skating at the roller rink at Whalom Park. At times it was just plain hard to find anybody at all.

&

That summer I was buzzing about UFOs to anyone who would listen. I had recently read two books that had stirred my imagination: *Incident at Exeter* and *The Interrupted Journey*, both by John Fuller. It wasn't just the subject matter that got me going; I liked the idea that the locations were somewhat local (New Hampshire). I was also reading magazines on the subject and even wrote a letter to one once criticizing it for doctoring an evidence picture for the sake of a cover layout—thus in effect—creating a hoax photo. They wholeheartedly concurred with me and to their credit even published my letter.

My boss at Thom McCann was named Gene. He was walking around the second floor checking stock in the same aisle that I was picking from and he stopped to chew the fat with me. Gene was in his early-forties (which at that time seemed very old to me) and he spoke with the accent of his native NYC. Inevitably, as it so often did with me in those days, the subject turned to flying saucers. He told me that even though he had never seen one himself, he still had a story to tell.

With my interest now piqued, I leaned on my cart while he perched on a pallet of wing tips to relate his tale. It was a hot and humid afternoon in the non-air-conditioned building and sweat beaded on his oily face and plastered his thinning black hair to his scalp. A crack of heat lightning was his cue to commence.

&

Back in the 1950s he had been an MP in the USAF, stationed at White Sands AFB in New Mexico and assigned to the graveyard shift. His patrol took him around the primary base and also out to the canteens, some of which were in the desert in the base's farthest reaches. One of the stops along the way was Charlie's—perhaps the most remote. He had planned to shoot the breeze with Charlie and get a cup of coffee but when he came near, he noticed that all of the lights were out. He now approached the canteen with caution, parking his jeep and drawing his service-issue, lightly-oiled, Colt .45 automatic. He went into the building—the only sound was the squealing of the spring on the screen door.

"Hey Charlie, you in there?" he'd stage-whispered in his New York accent, sweeping the shaft of the flashlight and muzzle of the .45 in tandem through the darkness. Then he heard a noise—like a mouse—from behind the lunch counter and went around to investigate. The flashlight's beam fell upon the concession owner himself, cowering under the lowest shelf of the counter. Staring up at the barrel of the .45 seemed to revive him and he got to his feet, relieved but obviously still shaken. Gene asked him what had happened.

Charlie explained that he had heard a crackling/buzzing sound outside and had gone out onto the porch to investigate, still wearing an apron and carrying the dish towel that he'd been drying the cups with. He looked out into the desert and at first didn't see anything, but looking up, noticed that a section of the stars in the sky were not visible as if they were blocked by a rectangular shape that was growing rapidly in size. The leading edge, now illuminated by the light from the building, inched towards his face and hovered only yards away. He could now discern that the surface was made of a dull grey substance like scuffed pot metal. From what he could make out the object was about the size of a football field hovering above the cooling desert. He had broken, run, switched off the lights and assumed a fetal position under his counter for two hours where he lay terrified until the Sergeant showed up and he had told his story. Gene had gone out onto the porch and shined his light up into the sky but saw nothing but stars.

෯

*Coda:*

    *My boss ended his story with a shrugging gesture as to what it all meant, and the clouds that had been withholding their hot rain relieved themselves. Gene went back to doing what he had been doing which meant that I needed to do the same thing. Wing tips were not moving that year but sandals from India were.*

*Jimmy's brother John*

# HOMERS

**That pigeon coop was built** for the ages. Jimmy's brother Johnny had worked alongside his carpenter father to build the sturdy little structure. It had a door, a paned window, perches, clapboard siding and proper roof shingles. It sat in their back yard next to the clothesline and if it was a little bit larger someone could have lived in it. Instead, it was occupied by its intended inhabitants: Johnny's homing pigeons.

Johnny had raised them and nurtured them, giving them their freedom once a day when they would spread their grey wings and majestically circle the neighborhood. It was an exhilarating sight the first time when he wondered if they were gone for good. But they repaid his faith by returning to roost on schedule. Johnny had showed me how you could hypnotize one by holding it in the palm of one hand and moving the index finger of the other hand up to its eyes and back repeatedly until when you released your grip, the bird would just lay there immobilized. He could even mimic their sound: *"cucKOO-wha-wha."*

&

Some months later I was walking up Gordon Avenue and I had heard the distinctive *pak* report of a BB gun which seemed to emanate from Jimmy's back yard. I heard it again as I approached and went over to investigate. It seemed to be coming from the bulkhead entrance to the cellar. As I went over I noticed that the yard was littered with pigeon carcasses in random postures of death.

I pushed open the bulkhead door to find Johnny splayed out across the top steps to the cellar, holding an air rifle to his shoulder. He had pushed it through a small hole that he had cut in the door that was just big enough to accommodate the barrel of the gun with a little space above for drawing a bead. I looked at his face and it was hard to read his feelings. I had to ask what he was doing. He explained that he had just grown tired of the pigeons and had released his flock for one last fly-over of the neighborhood. While they were circling he had scattered bread crusts all over the yard and then taken up position in his sniper's nest. When his flock returned they saw the bread and lit to eat some. It was to be their last meal for as they did, he methodically dispatched them one-by-one until the job was done. It had taken him all morning.

&

*Coda:*

*Pigeons always slumped on my family's roof. They nestled as best they could in the eaves of the house clinging to it as if it was a sacred shrine. Perhaps a prior resident had kept them as a hobby and either lost interest or moved away. Those birds and their descendants had been there ever since. They were there watching us when my mother and I drove away from the house for the last time and I had asked if she wanted to take a last look. She said, "No, let's just go." She'd had enough of that house, but for all I know the pigeons are still there. They are homers after all.*

*Fitchburg, Massachusetts, 1911*

# PAPERMAKER

*Prelude:*

*Hugh M. Gallagher, 68, of 34 Sprague Street, a retired papermaker, died last night at Fitchburg General Hospital after a short illness. A native of Ireland, he came to this city forty-nine years ago. He was employed as a papermaker for many years at Crocker Burbank Co. retiring two years ago. He was a member of the local Aerie of Eagles... (It goes on the list the survivors and the funeral arrangements.)—Memorial obituary from the Fitchburg Sentinel dated July 28, 1958.*

&

**I keep my grandfather's obituary** in my sock drawer. The laminated coating did not stop the clipping from becoming amber with age. As I come across these little prayer cards and remembrances, I find it interesting that the funeral homes have names of the same nationality as the deceased—in this case Mallahey. The immigrant groups were sticking together to the end and giving a brother the business.

I can remember my mother dressing for her father's wake, still displaying the beauty of her youth at the age of 38. She looked glamorous with her red hair finally unbound from bobby pins and wearing her black dress which tonight would be for mourning.

Looking more like she should be going to the Academy Awards than this somber occasion, she primped for my mirror but also talked me through things as she did. I tried to process my first bitter taste of grief: the grip of the stomach, the lump in the throat and the tears that fill the eyes but don't fall. Although I rarely saw him, the sobering fact that I would never get another chance began to sink in.

Occasionally I stayed with Nana (Hannah) and Grandpa (Hugh) in West Fitchburg. On one of these visits he took me to work with him to see the paper being made. We went through the stations of the process, and I leaned over the huge vats filled with pulp and water while he explained what was happening. All of the men, including my grandfather, were wearing self-made skullcaps of paper—the badge of the papermaker. They made one for me too, as I was an honorary papermaker for the day.

Nana and Grandpa had 11 children. My mother named me after a brother who had died young in an automobile accident: John Vincent Gallagher. Grandpa had not wanted John to have a car for reasons of his own, so the son purchased one secretly and parked it down the street from the big company-owned house on Baltic Lane so that his father would not know. Over time he parked it closer and closer to the house every night and eventually Grandpa grudgingly accepted it. Handsome John Vincent, an aspiring stage actor, died in the convertible that he had so coveted. The rollover accident took place at the intersection of Ashburnham Street and Westminster Hill Road. The gruesome detail of the accident is that he was decapitated in the crash. I drive through it whenever I visit and make the sign-of-the-cross. As was the custom at the time, the body lay-in-state in the front parlor of the family house. I try to imagine the siblings tiptoeing around the house with their brother in the front room and I cannot.

The paper mills were nestled in along the granite banks of the river and its tributaries. Water seemed to run everywhere in West Fitchburg with its warrens of workingman's houses perched on its steep hills. Huge wooden pipes, bound by steel rods, crisscrossed the chasms connecting the magic ingredient—water—to the factories and their pulp.

It was a hardscrabble existence especially during the Depression and then the war. The Gallagher children grew up standing up for themselves and maybe were well aware of the attitudes that some members of the Fitchburg community held towards their working-class Irish status as well as their Roman Catholic faith. Perhaps with good reason then, the neighborhood has a slogan that belies a chip-on-the-shoulder mentality, "West Fitchburg Against The World!" When the oldest boys, Edward and Raymond, were of age, they joined the Navy and shipped off to fight in the war; Edward to the Atlantic, Raymond to the Pacific. Their sisters found work as maids for the well-to-do or waited on tables.

By necessity, Grandpa could be a strict disciplinarian. He had a razor strop hanging in the bathroom that was used on more than one occasion for something other than sharpening his straight-razor (or so I've been told). When he grew angry, his voice rose in pitch as well as volume and he became a true Irish tenor (something I can hear in my own voice from time-to-time). He held court at dinner with all of those kids in his sway. When he made a cogent point, he would pound the table with his fist making the *Blue Willow* dishes rattle and in his Irish-lilted tenor roar, "Am I right or am I wrong?" His children would answer without a pause, "You're right, Pops," in perfect unison.

*Marcia, David, Janice and me*

# SHOWDOWN

**One hot summer day**, when I was still quite young, the Gallagher clan gathered for a cookout in the backyard of the big house on Baltic Lane. The family now included grandchildren of which I was one of many (the number eventually swelled to 13 by the time he had passed away although they continued coming after Grandpa was gone). It was a rare occasion to have so many of the family gathered in one place at one time.

Grandpa liked to tease the little ones and this particular day he was amusing himself with a fly swatter. Every time one of us little kids would walk by, we would feel its sting on our backsides. When faced with our indignation, he would feign innocence and explain that there had been a fly on us. This went on for quite a while until, to paraphrase the Cisco Kid's sidekick Pancho, "enough was too much."

I wheeled away from him rubbing my butt and stepped a few paces back. The family grew quiet, sensing that a showdown was nigh. At this juncture I should describe my attire for this confrontation; that would be a black cowboy hat, black cowboy boots, worn with my undershorts and with two six-guns strapped to my waist. I looked a little like that Naked Cowboy in Times Square at the age of five. My hands now hovered over my holstered cap guns in the classic stance of the gunfighter, but rather than slap leather, I fusilladed him with words, "Grandpa, you're a son-of-a-bitch!"

He was gobsmacked, as was the whole family. *Someone had spoken back to Pops!* You could have heard a pin drop during that pause until my mother swooped over, said something conciliatory to Grandpa, and then dragged her little gunslinger over to the watermelon table by the wrist where she probably gave me some stern words about language usage and with whom to use it. The Gallagher clan that had become wax statues for a few minutes began to reanimate. This exchange made me a legend in my family—at least for a little while. My 15 minutes of Gallagher fame, so-to-speak.

In the last years of Nana's life, my mother would move in with her for part of the month so that they could stretch their Social Security checks. I didn't remember the *SOB* incident and I got the story from my mother but Nana would tell it to me every single time she saw me. She loved it so.

&

*Coda:*

*Grandpa died two years after retiring. In his time here he had changed nationalities at 19, found a job secure enough to raise 11 children through the Depression and the War and steeped them in the Roman Catholic faith. By extension he made my own life possible. In my favorite memory of him he is trying to get a laugh out of me by donning an old-fashioned derby hat, sitting in a chair and blowing on his thumb. He would lean back on his chair, pressing the hard brim of the derby against the wall until it would flip up. The illusion was that blowing on his thumb made the hat pop up. It was very Chaplinesque.*

*"Duckeye" and me at Whitney Field*

# WHITNEY FIELD

**On the floodplain of the** Nashua River, where Nipmucks, Nashways and French Hill hellions once roamed, now stand the assorted big-box chain stores of what is called the Whitney Field Mall. When first built, it had been named the Searstown Mall after its anchor franchise. But perhaps a wave of nostalgia had passed through the Plastic City since I had last visited. Now it bears the name of the recreational area that once existed on a portion of that land. In summer it had been a mecca for a few generations of Hill kids.

☙

At the dawn of the mall era, developers and city fathers looked to cashing in on the trend. With large tracts of land at a premium, other options were put on the table. One plan was to build the new stores downtown, infilling around the existing collection of Victorian commercial structures, thus preserving them as well as downtown shopping. The proposal was placed before the citizens—including the display of an architect's model of how it would all work—but in the end it was rejected.

When they went back to the old drawing board in 1965, they took a harder look at Whitney Field. The land had been a gift to the City of Leominster for use by its children in the year 1935. The benefactor's name was Fred A. Whitney—a prosperous area industrialist. There were eight more acres in the endowment but never with the apparent intention of that land being built upon. A casual observer might draw the conclusion that building on it was not feasible anyway due to its proximity to the river and the low-lying topography.

On closer scrutiny of the '35 agreement, it was discovered that the words *"In Perpetuity"* were nowhere to be found in the document. The planners decided that after 30 years, the *"Frogines"* had paddled around enough and now it was the big peoples' turn to play. Mr. Whitney might have done a few rotations in his grave had he known that his generous gift was being "regifted."

&

When I ran there, Whitney Field stood on a solid, dry pair of acres in a corner of the parcel. There was a large chlorine-bombarded pool with a diving board, a tall diving platform and a separate baby pool. All of the usual equipment dotted the sandy playground. You accessed it by foot descending 102 cement stairs at Sixth Street down the valley wall to follow the fire road—or went the long way to the access road on Spring Street—which was better if you were on your bike. The first time I was first there, in the mid-Fifties, a rather ornate Victorian-style wooden structure that everybody called the *Pavilion* was still standing from the old days.

It always felt a little remote and under-supervised down there, so it wasn't hard for somebody to decide one night that the *Pavilion* would make a nice bonfire and they burned it spectacularly to the ground. Because of its location, it would take a bit of time for the Fire Department to be alerted to the blaze so these firebugs knew they could take their sweet time and enjoy the spectacle of their doings. The whirling bats, barn swallows and a bullfrog or two would be the only other witnesses—and they wouldn't be talking.

That *Pavilion* was replaced by a more utilitarian structure with a shingled roof supported by steel posts with low cinder block walls that housed the Ping-Pong tables, basketballs and so forth. It was also called the *Pavilion* and it was built to withstand a nuclear blast.

One of the pieces of playground equipment was a 50-foot-tall steel pipe that had rotation hub at the top with four chains attached that ended in handles like little ladders. It was sort of an industrial-strength maypole. If you could get four kids together to run around it pulling the chains, you could get up enough speed to leave the ground. One day a bunch of guys who were too old for this shit, invited me over for a go-around. One of them was Frankie's older brother Danny.

I felt honored to be accepted as a big kid and I grabbed onto a handle as instructed. They had put a twist on the game though—they had crossed my chain over the next for extra lift—and then off we went.

Almost immediately my feet left the ground as my chain whiplashed me over the chain I had crossed, propelling me over Danny's shoulders and up into an angle of 60 degrees—pretty high off the ground. Everybody looked kind of small from my vantage point, but I had a great view of the playground and the pool. I was way up there man.

Suddenly I realized that the real reason they had called me over was that they needed someone light who would go higher and that the real game they were playing was to get that someone to let go of the handle and hurtle to his doom. They pulled the chains around as fast as they could, chanting maniacally, "jump, jump, jump," and grinning up at me like rabid jackals. But there was no way that I was going to do that out of fear—and even though centrifugal force *tore both Buster Browns right off my feet*—I clung to that bar for dear life itself. Out of pity, guilt, respect or fatigue, they eventually gave up pulling and I gratefully returned to earth.

In time we became the big kids we once dreaded, but I like to think that we were a kinder, gentler breed of hoodlum. I'm sure we exercised our seniority in the pecking order, but after all, the Rat thing was mostly for show, to be honest.

The pool still beckoned but fewer kids seemed to heed its call. The equipment fell into disrepair and the Spring Street access road was littered dangerously with broken glass. The last summer that I spent any time there, some attractive college girls were working as counselors/lifeguards. They seemed to be a cut above us and had a manner that bespoke an upbringing on the far side of the tracks. In a conversation with one of them I ridiculed our contemporary nemeses, the Lunchies, as conformists, dressing identically as they did. She countered that *we* in fact were the true conformists, dressed identically in black leather jackets, dungarees and engineer boots like we were wearing uniforms. Although I hated to admit it, suddenly my long-held stance seemed obsolete. This was the summer of 1963 and it may have been the turning point when I began to let go of my carefully cultivated Fifties persona and accept the times in which I lived.

*Coda:*

*I had a teacher at Leominster High School who once referred to Whiney Field as being "the biggest breeding ground for juvenile delinquency" the Plastic City had ever known. I thought that he might be directing that at me and I felt a complex mixture of embarrassment and pride at the same time. This entity that had been such a factor in my childhood closed for good in 1965. It seemed eternal at the time but in fact it was only there for 30 years.*

*Jeddah, 1988*

# THE KINGDOM

**The departure terminal at** Kennedy was vast and alive with travelers who flowed through myriad paths toward their respective destinations like blood cells through arteries. Mine would eventually lead me to The Kingdom of Saudi Arabia where I'd been assigned to a job by my company for what was proposed to be a nine-month commitment. With my larger suitcase conveying to the hold of the 747, I was toting a duffle in one hand and Fender Stratocaster in a retro tweed case in the other. Along with the usual detritus associated with travel, the duffle held my recently purchased Eric Clapton retrospective *Crossroads* as well as a Sony Rockman. The way I saw it, I would have some time to improve as a guitarist on my off time in the KSA. There would be little to distract me from practicing. It was a dry country and I'd be there on a bachelor-basis without the responsibilities or comforts of home. Socially I'd be placing myself into exile one might say. The only television was the closed-circuit system of the company's compound which broadcast video cassettes recorded from network programming back in the states and those might be evenings of ten-year-old situation comedies.

The brightest spot on compound TV was *The Today Show* which was up to date daily even if we would get it a five in the evening. I figured I would do my job, return to the compound, take a swim, fix something to eat and settle in for an hour or two of practicing along with my Clapton tapes. After nine months of that I might just give "Slowhand" a run for his money. Just kidding about that last part.

&

As we inched slowly through security, I scanned the terminal out of boredom. Out of all these hundreds of people one figure stood out. From the far side a big heavyset kid seemed to be locked on to me. He had shaggy bleached-blond hair sticking out at odd angles from under a baseball hat worn backwards. Even at that distance he was obvious down to his huge unlaced sneakers. My first thought was that he looked like a musician.

When I got to the screener he opened the case and pulled the sunburst electric out for a look. There was a hubbub behind me that made me turn around in curiosity. A dozen people in line behind me were smiling and laughing with each other as if in relief. Seeing my questioning expression someone said, "We thought it was a rifle case." I guess it must have spooked them. When I turned back around the husky blond kid was looking at the guitar and asking if he could check it out to which I obliged. He must have made a bee line across the terminal at the sight of the Fender.

Once through security, I hunkered down to wait for the nonstop Saudia flight to Jeddah, KSA. The Kingdom would be dry, in all ways, this I knew, and for me that was no laughing matter. I'd said my farewells at home and now it was time to do the same to the grape and the grain. I sat at the airport bar with my toe touching the guitar case and put back a Sambuca and a pair of Heinekens. Then there was my boarding call. *Arrivederci* Sambuca, *Tot ziens* Heiniken. Parting is such sweet sorrow.

The flight attendants were all female and wore navy blue suits both crisp and businesslike. The first two I encountered had high cheekbones, black eyes, full lips and actually looked enough alike to be sisters. I took pains to inform them that my baby needed to be safe and they assured me that they would keep an eye on it.

Glancing around the cabin the first thing that I noticed were the bottles of drinking water on the passengers' trays. They had this way of serving it so that the cap still partially dangled from the opened bottles. No nips served on this bad boy. There seemed to be less than 50 souls aboard the enormous airplane; men, women and children—everybody dressed in western-style garb as far as I could see—and all heading home.

I took my seat perhaps 11 rows back in the business class section and towards the center. As we taxied to the take-off position, rather than flight safety instructions on the screen, two hands appeared palms up like reading a book. Arabic prayers began to intone from the sound system and I had my first "Not-In-Kansas-Anymore" moment. To my left sat a somewhat elderly white-haired gentleman in a summer weight suit. Through the small talk I learned that he was an American medical doctor working in the Kingdom. He dispensed tips on living in Saudi Arabia to which I listened attentively. "This is not like living in Europe," he said, "this is a totally different type of culture so be prepared for some shock." He didn't lay it on thick, but with the economy of an elder the message boiled down to taking what was there for me but to keep my eyes open for trouble—and avoiding it.

Once the jumbo jet levelled-off he got up to search for a place in the mostly empty plane to stretch out for the long night flight and advised me to do the same. "These are nocturnal people and they can make a racket at night," he warned. I told him thanks but stayed put as he made his way back into the shadows of the cavernous, darkened cabin. I got comfortable where I was and dozed off sitting down.

∞

Above the hiss/hum of the engines voices had begun to rise. It seemed to be in my dream to begin with. Angry Arabic words were being spoken and although unintelligible to me, their intent seemed clear. It sounded like a political rally with a main speaker blustering rhetoric while supporters cheered him on. My eyes flickered open and at first it looked like the choppy frames of a silent movie. The lights were dimmer now than they were when I'd nodded off.

The rally was down in front of the screen where the prayerful hands had been shown. I feigned being more asleep than I actually was until I could get a handle on what was happening, and I squinted at the proceedings like a restless dreamer. Off to the right a smallish man with a loud voice stood on his seat and shouted—clearly wound up. Through my dropped eyelids I could see that he was pointing back at me and his cheering section was looking back in my direction too. Most of these guys were young and they seemed more amused by the speaker than anything, but he obviously was trying to whip them into a frenzy. I was catching enough of the gist to know that the subject was people from outside the country going there to work.

At one point he walked up the aisle to row to where I still played possum and said for effect in perfect English that, "They don't *give a shit, man.*" I know that he knew I must be faking sleep and was trying to prod me into a confrontation but I didn't take the bait. I did know if he came down the row toward me the possum would have to fuck up his whole day— lynch mob or not. He rejoined his audience and continued his harangue for a while longer but in time it petered-out.

I fell back into an uneasy slumber as the cabin lights were dimmed to nothing. It had become late and only starlight and moonlight shafted in through the windows. In my imagination assassins were low-crawling up the aisles toward me, serpentine daggers clenched in their rotting teeth. In a moonbeam I saw a bearded man in ballooning pants, pointed sandals with a turban wrapped around his head. Could that be a scimitar stuck in his sash I wondered? I felt like I'd seen him in an old *Popeye* cartoon about "Sinbad the Sailor", but at that irrational moment I feared he might be coming for my head. It was a troubled sleep until morning I'd have to admit.

When I opened my eyes again it was the sun that shafted in through the cabin windows filling it with an almost painful brilliance. There were still people down where the mob had assembled the previous evening, but the group had transformed in nature. Many of the women had changed into black *abayas* and were attending to their children alongside their husbands. The families were interacting in a warm, convivial fashion. I saw the assassin from the Popeye cartoon but now he was just a white-bearded grandpa in loose-fitting clothes almost like pajamas. Not a soul paid me the slightest bit of attention as we began our descent into Abdul Aziz Airport.

&#8474;

*Coda:*

*As we deplaned I arranged to get my Strat from the flight attendants, grabbed my bag and fumbled up the aisle. When I stepped off the 747 and onto the skyway I caught the first whiff of my new home—burning sand on a hellacious wave of heat. As fortune would have it, my tormentor from the previous evening was right in front of me in line. I was so close I could smell the goop in his hair. I had a couple of inches on him and considered pulling him over once inside the terminal and giving him what we used to call in the Plastic City an "object lesson."*

*But in the end, I denied myself the pleasure, heeding the good doctor's advice about avoiding trouble. It wouldn't do to be arrested on my first day in this strange, unpredictable new world.*

*A rebel fully realized, 1962*

# DUEL OF THE TITANS

**...was what was showing** at the Whalom Drive-In the night
Geno, Carl and I snuck in over the fence at the back of the
parking area. Even if we had the price of a ticket, it just seemed
stupid to buy one and walk into a drive-in. Drive-in—get it?
Whalom Drive-In was so named because of its proximity to the
amusement park and lake down the street. In the year to come,
we'd be sneaking in stashed in the trunk of our friend Ray's
finny Ford—but for now—we just hoofed it.

*Duel of the Titans* was a risible sword-and-sandal epic
from Italy with hilariously inept dubbed-in English. It starred
Gordon "Tarzan" Scott and Steve "Hercules" Reeves in what
might charitably be described as an "imaginative" retelling of
the founding of the city of Rome (Romulus, Remus, wolves
blah blah blah). Geno lifted weights in those days and Steve
Reeves was his body-building idol.

We wandered around trying to find one of those pole-mounted aluminum speakers that worked so that we could listen to some "dialogue." There were a lot to choose from because people interested in the movie were parked up front. Patrons in the sparse assortment of cars parked towards the rear had a different agenda and we knew enough to give them a wide berth. At the intermission we walked down to the concession stand to spend what we'd saved on the admission to buy hot dogs and cokes. Little did we know that we were walking into an ambush. Apparently the staff had been monitoring our movements and were probably arranging to go to the back of the parking lot to nab us until we conveniently walked into their hands.

The cinder block bunker that served as both a projection booth and concession stand was at the middle of the complex. We had not even entered the building when we were overtaken by a mob of angry adults. There were at least six and possibly eight who sprang out and jumped us. Each of us had a bear hug locked on him and we in turn did our best to break free. Burly Geno windmilled his big arms, broke from his captor's grip and lumbered off (tellingly, no one chased after him). Skinny Carl did a little squatting maneuver, dropped from his attacker's hold and blasted away like the Road Runner (beeeooooowwww)—gone in three seconds. That left the entire mob to devote total attention to me. As I was overcome I became vividly aware of the yellow light bulb over the entrance, its clear fixture full of dead moths.

This mad scrum burst into the lobby, shouting and struggling, and the customers and staff turned to watch. I became aware of one guy who was screaming louder than the rest and realized that I had seen him in the past: the manager. He was a tall man wearing a grey plaid suit, his hair grey on the sides but gone on top. As we jostled through the room, I saw him position himself to deliver a solid punch to the side of my head. My hands were totally pinned and I have to say; he got me pretty good. That one did hurt.

When we got to a certain point, they released me and shoved me up against a poster for *Hatari!* in an aluminum wall case. Even John Wayne looked alarmed squinting down at this drama from his poster. Though I was still captive, my hands were now free and I put them up in self-defense and started firing off a few shots of my own. The *Duke* had my back.

Eventually a Lunenburg cop broke through the mob and the onlookers. He grabbed me by the arm and yanked me out and into the night. As we walked towards the drive-in exit, the din from the concession stand began to recede into the distance but suddenly the manager sprang out of nowhere and started screaming at me again. Looks like he had enjoyed smashing me in the head the first time so much he'd have another shot. Even the cop seemed dumfounded.

A young father with a small child on his hip had apparently been watching this whole sordid incident with contempt. He'd been shadowing us all the way out. He got into the manager's face and told him in no uncertain terms to shut up and get back inside, pointing the way for him. The manager, stunned, did as he was told. The cop escorted me out and told me not to sneak in any more. I said okay that I wouldn't and I walked down Route 13 towards the park in a night as quiet as a tomb and as black as death. Geno and Carl had been waiting for me near a closed ice cream stand while trying to figure out how to bust me loose. I gave them obligatory hell for running out on me but I wasn't really pissed-off at all—I would have done the same thing. I even managed to quip, "I was never so happy to see a cop coming at me," rubbing my sore jaw.

⅋

The apartment over my mother's house was vacant and we snuck up to sleep for what was left of the night. We staked out corners of our own but as the night grew colder we migrated to the bathroom where the hot water pipe and our combined body temperatures were enough to warm the room. We slept on the floor like puppies until the morning when my mother had yelled up from downstairs waking us up. Carl's mother had called looking for him. Carl was in trouble.

&#8667;

*Coda:*

*My memory of this incident is of aluminum grey: the screen, the speakers, the manager's suit and hair. In the ensuing years I often drove by nursing revenge fantasies, but time exacted its own brand of vengeance. The drive-in closed to business and weeds grew through the cracks in the tar of the idle parking area. The screen stood unused for years, a last testament to the theater's existence, gradually falling apart until it was finally razed completely. The manager, the hot dogs, the Pic mosquito repellent, the dead moths, the posters in their cases and the death-black night have become nothing more than a memory for me and a story to tell you.*

*In times following that incident, we would hang out with a friend named Ray who had a car and, yes, as I confessed earlier, we used to sneak into the drive-in hiding in the trunk to save money.*

*Ray was a year ahead of me in school and although I didn't know him at the time, he was in the concession stand on the night of the* Duel of the Titans *incident. He had been in the crowd of onlookers when I was backed up against the John Wayne poster in my Marlon Brando jacket, throwing punches back at the angry mob. Ray said it was the coolest thing he had ever seen.*

*Young warrior, Hampton Beach, 1950s*

# A GRENADE IN THE GARDEN

*Prelude:*
*I no longer make my home in the Plastic City, but there is enough of the place stamped on my DNA that I still feel the tug of its gravity. I will always pause at the rare mention of Leominster in the Boston-area media. They are often trivial-sounding affairs typical of a small town that mostly make you chuckle and shake your head. There also might be motor vehicle mishaps, small crimes or domestic violence—not pleasant, yet I attend with interest nonetheless.*

&#x200B;

**Some years back a lady** was puttering in her garden, somewhere on French Hill, when her trowel made contact with something hard in the soil. "Another rock," she thought and began to unearth the object. She laid a potato-sized, sod-encrusted clump into the palm of her hand and, after wiping it off, froze in terror. This was no bolder, it was a bomb of some kind—a military hand grenade. She set it down gingerly then ran into her house to dial 9-1-1. The appropriate resources arrived punctually and *en masse*. Fire trucks and police Crown Vics sounded their sirens and flashed their light bars. The bomb-sniffing German Shepherd was first deployed followed by a bumbling bomb disposal robot that looked like it had come from the *Sharper Image* catalog. In the end it fell upon a poor slob in a bomb-proof suit to complete the job. As the curtain fell on this two-hour drama, the object was declared nonthreatening. Although it was indeed a hand grenade (an MK2 fragmentation device from the WWII/Korea era, to be precise), it was devoid of its fuse as well as the two ounces of TNT that could easily spoil someone's day. A dummy in other words, and since no battles had occurred on French Hill as far as anyone could recall, how it had gotten into those Petunias was declared "a mystery."

&

## The War Lover

I have always loved war. There, someone said it. Not the kind in which people actually die, but rather as portrayed on the silver screen, television, comic books and in my imagination. People (boys) who claim otherwise may not be forthcoming. When I was young, I saw the excitement rather than the tragedy and human cost. Stories centered on WWII were ubiquitous in my youth, a gift of the landscape so to speak. A lot of the films were made as morale-boosting, flag-waving entertainment for our parents' generation (The Greatest) but were recycled for ours. After all, you've got to have product to pack the two theaters in town (the Plymouth and the "Met") on Saturday afternoons. Therefore: along with the half-dozen cartoons, *Flash Gordon, the Three Stooges, the Coming Attractions* and a monster movie: who cares if they threw in *Thirty Seconds Over Tokyo (1944)* to round out the bill? It was still a lot of bang for your quarter-buck. As far back as the early-Sixties my mother perceptively observed, "Without World War Two what would they make

126

movies about?" Do the studios not remain at it to this day?

Those old films were also broadcast in the afternoon on local television so I knew some of them like the back of my hand. I could quote from *Bataan, They Were Expendable, A Walk in the Sun, Stalag 17* or *From Here to Eternity.* On TV there were: *Combat, Citizen Soldier, Victory At Sea* and more. My comics of choice were *Sergeant Rock and Easy Company, Gunner and Sarge and Jeb Stuart and the Haunted Tank.* Copying those great illustrators was my inspiration to go into Art as a profession… for what it was worth.

All of this may have instilled in me (and by extension my generation) a sense of dedication to country, a code-of-honor and examples of the nature of courage. One might muse that we were being primed for Viet Nam by spillover from the patriotic fervor of the Forties. We were young then, and brave, and never more so than after an afternoon at the movies.

We broke into teams: one ran off into the woods to set up an ambush while the other waited and counted to a hundred before embarking on a pursuit. We'd be armed to teeth too. My generous parents bought me toys at my whim and these were usually rifles and pistols of every shape and size, so I became the de-facto armorer of the gang.

With knotted stomachs the groups would approach each other until the moment of conflict, then, after a barrage of BANG-BANG-BANG, we would settle down to argue about who had really killed whom.

Another great game was "Best Falls" where we rehearsed colorful ways to die. The premise was: if you were "IT" you got to call the weapon that would be used to kill the other players as they paraded by unawares. "IT" would judge which player had died the best then that person would become the new "IT" entitling him to choose the next implement of destruction. We all got pretty good at dying after a while.

**Giving the Devil His Due**

Germany was our enemy in WWII. Our fathers and uncles battled the *Wehrmacht* and *Luftwaffe* across Europe. The Nazis were monsters and Hitler was mad. But I've got grudging respect for the Third Reich's branding. Maybe it was *Der Fuhrer's* art school background, but they conceived a brilliant identity package. After my years as a graphic designer for a major corporation, I can appreciate their visual concept—if not their philosophy. Former Corporal Schicklgruber and his principal designer, Herr Speer, no doubt spent endless hours designing a "look" for the *Tausendjähriges Reich* from the ground up. I can imagine them tweaking the color of that twisted cross logo, or bickering about the appropriate use of those Art Deco eagles. I had the uniforms and weapons so well memorized that I can draw them accurately to this day.

※

**An Epiphany**

One hot Sunday in 1960, with nothing to do and nobody to hang out with, I went to Metropolitan Theater on a whim. The poster that lured me in was for a documentary film called *Mein Kamph*. It looked a little academic but I figured I would be seeing a lot of action and cool weaponry—and after all—I had begun to think of myself as a subject-matter expert so this might further my education in this area.

The film flickered to life for me alone in that crumbling relic that had once been a palace-of-light. As the Americans moved east and the Russians moved west, the usual footage of burning tanks, flak-dodging planes and fleeing refugees played out—but there was a difference: images of the dead. This is what they did not show on TV. As *Mein Kamph* drew to a close, it documented the liberation of the concentration camps with their populace of living skeletons—the *lucky* ones. One indelible image was that of a stack of naked female corpses being bulldozed into a mass grave. You could see how they styled their hair and how some wore makeup, others eyeglasses. That image has haunted me for a long time, and I never looked at war as being anything but ugly and tragic from that day onward.

&

**Case Closed?**

We had a spirited game of "Hide-and-Go-Seek" going on one summer day, long before *Mein Kamph*. It was playing out over several back yards on Tenth Street mostly behind Wayne's house. I ran over to hide behind someone's backyard incinerator and made an astounding discovery: a cache of hand grenades—at least a dozen of them. I called out to the gang, "Hey guys, grenades…GRENADES!" They all came running and we scooped them up as fast as we could. A guy still dressed in his Army uniform—one of the many servicemen that lived on French Hill—came out of his house and yelled at us to get out of there which we did—but not without our crop of pineapples.

On closer scrutiny, it was obvious that they weren't dangerous. The rings and cotter pins were missing as were the "spoons," fuses and powder. In fact they were hollow. They were painted blue and we deduced that they were used for training on Fort Devens. As to why that guy brought them home is anybody's guess. We lobbed them at each other all summer but eventually they dispersed and disappeared. One graced my bookcase for years, but even that one vanished in time. For all I know, a grenade may even have ended up in some lady's Petunia patch.

&

*Coda*

*This was supposed to be an amusing little story about lost and found hand grenades and how they got there, but it became more of a discourse on war than I had intended it to. As I've said in the past, the stories dictate how they will be told. There is some somber material mixed in with some humor that I hope doesn't offend anyone. I have the highest regard for those who served our nation and mourn the loss of the innocent victims of the nightmare of war.*

129

*G.I. Blues, 1967*

# SEASON OF WAR

**The year was 1967 and** the season of war had come around again. It seems that there was a meat grinder in Southeast Asia called Viet Nam (which nobody had ever heard of) that was putting a lot of 19-year-olds into new wardrobes. Before the year was up I'd be "wearin' the green" myself and not just on St. Patrick's Day. This would, however, necessitate a flight to Fort Bragg, North Carolina for a fitting.

I'd drawn a low number in the draft lottery, passed a pre-induction physical and kept finding ominous invitations from Uncle Sam in the mailbox. Even though I explained that I was planning to shampoo my hair that year, he was not allowing me to gracefully decline. Unless something came along to change things, I'd be going bye-bye and very shortly too. Some guys were running off to Canada to avoid the draft but I knew I couldn't do that—it actually sounded worse in a way. I asked my mother if I really *had* to go but she just shrugged her shoulders and reminded me that her brothers had served in WWII and did not wait to be drafted with patriotism running strong after Pearl Harbor. I guess I was hoping she would get me off-the-hook somehow: maybe call in and tell them I was sick or something. But after that conversation, I knew there was no hope. I was going.

❧

At that time I was playing bass in a band called the Cavemen. I'd originally gotten the gig by filling in for the rhythm guitarist, Mike, while he was taking six-months active duty training as part of his requirement for the Massachusetts Army National Guard. Mike had since returned but I stayed with the group anyway when Pete—the former bassist—left. The only catch being that I needed to learn to play bass. The drummer, Paul, keyboardist Dennis and new member Lenny were all in the same Guard unit as Mike: Company B, 26th Aviation Battalion, the Yankee Division drilling in the Plastic City. They said they would keep an eye out for an opening and sure enough one eventually did come along. These Guard positions were in high demand because of the unpopularity of that war and I was lucky to get a jump on the posting.

Now it was my turn in the barrel. The deal was; you'd take basic training and advanced individual training with the regular Army, but rather than being shipped off to exotic ports-of-call, you went home and settled in to fulfill your six-year commitment—one weekend a month at your armory and two weeks at Camp Drum, New York in the summer. My fellow Cavemen threw me the obligatory going-away drunken bash to ensure that I would be ghastly ill for my bus trip to Boston and my flight to DC with connecting flight to Fayetteville, North Carolina for some *hot fun in Joo-lie sun*. It was on this, my first flight ever, that I encountered Robert Kennedy.

❧

**RFK**

I'd seen Bobby and his brother Ted from the window of

the plane as they were boarding at Logan. They had so much luggage that they were personally supervising its loading into the hold. Although Bobby would not officially announce his candidacy for president until the following March, there was a lot of buzz about him following in his brother John's footsteps—something he would do in the most tragic way in June 1968.

To put the events into perspective, I should note that JFK was revered as a near-saint in our house. His campaign, nomination and ascension to the Oval Office was a thrill ride for my mother who could relate well to his upbringing in another large Irish-Catholic family from Massachusetts (major economic differences aside). She also found him handsome. Truth-be-known, I think she loved him.

I was home sick from school when JFK was shot. My mother and I were watching two different television stations as the news began to trickle out of Dallas. She would come to my room periodically to compare reports with me. Finality came when Walter Cronkite lifted the horn-rimmed glasses from his watery eyes, looked a clock on the wall and announced that the president had died at one p.m., Central Standard Time. It felt like a personal loss. My mother was shattered. Now Robert wore the Kennedy mantle and seemed destined to lead the country.

&

Once our jet leveled-off, Bobby appeared at the door to the first-class section and struck up a conversation with the coach passengers in the front rows—doing a little campaigning I suppose. I was 10 or so rows back and could not make out what was being said. I only heard sporadic bursts of laughter. RFK made the cabin electric. Standing during the entire flight in the doorway he never stopped smiling with those big Kennedy choppers as he chatted up the passengers. He appears now in my memory in vivid Technicolor; white button-down shirt with repp tie, blue eyes, tanned by the sun, threads of grey mixing in with the famous mop of auburn hair.

Bobby had sometimes come across as arrogant and tough in the media but it was nowhere in evidence that morning. He didn't return to his seat until it was announced that they were beginning the final approach to Dulles. With a small wave and a smile he was gone.

After landing in DC, Mooney—another Massachusetts guardsman heading down for basic—went off to get some travel information for the next leg of our journey to Fort Bragg while I stayed watching our bags. I was standing next to what seemed to be a mountain of brown leather suitcases. It turns out that it belonged to the Kennedy entourage; for left guarding that stack was none other than the astronaut and Kennedy running-buddy, John Glenn—first American to orbit the earth. Glenn was a huge celebrity and national hero in those years and it seemed a little demeaning in my eyes to make someone of that stature stand there like a goon watching the luggage (well, like I was). He noticed me looking in his direction and I would swear he seemed a little embarrassed.

❦

*Coda:*

*There is a famous photograph of Robert Kennedy's bleeding head being cradled by a busboy the kitchen of the Ambassador Hotel as his life seeped out of him. It always makes me think of Abraham Lincoln. In my memory of that July day of the flight to Washington, I see him as he looked on the plane, bathed in brilliant sunlight. It was like seeing Lincoln alive again, standing, smiling and chatting in the doorway to first-class, all in vivid Technicolor.*

*New Castle, New Hampshire, 1979*

# MONORAIL

*Prelude:*

*The monorail was once a futuristic vision of travel but a kind of pie-in-the-sky. It is something that you might now see in a Disney-created environment, but not many other places as far as I can tell. It's a train, dangling from a support and it's all very high-tech and probably practical, yet in the actual world, there don't seem to be many in service. Years ago I was reading an old* Popular Mechanics *article at a used book store that postulated that by the year 1972 we'd all be commuting to work via personal helicopter.*

&

**Picture if you will**, a man, driving down a seemingly endless stretch of highway through an open expanse of desert. It is twilight and the gloom has begun to gather but not enough so he has to turn on the headlights. The sky to his right is red near the horizon, the few elongated clouds are purple and the distant mesas appear black. His car leaves something to be desired. It is more than few years-old and he tells his mechanic that he is hoping to get one more year out of it. The mechanic smirks and replies that he hears that a lot. At the moment though the car is running strongly but he listens for problem sounds and worries about that left rear tire.

He and his wife have grown tired of bickering for the day and she now sits in blessed silence, her head turned away from him, lolling into sleep with a rivulet of drool seeping from her lips. The children who have been pestering each other have also fallen silent and he can see in the rearview mirror that at least one of them is sound asleep nestled in the squalid detritus of a dinner served from a drive-thru window.

This stretch of highway parallels a monorail track. In his boredom he looks up at a train that matches his pace. With the sun setting behind it, the cars are cast in shadow but the interiors are illuminated. The passengers are not sitting in seats but rather milling around the space as if at a cocktail party. The centerpiece of the car is as an enormous *Balthazar* of Champagne apparently on top of a low table of some sort.

He sees that the women are attractive and nicely-dressed. As they converse through their smiles they gesture by pushing their hair away from their faces or tossing it back over their shoulders. The men are wearing expensive-looking jackets or suits worn with their shirts open at the throat. They all have fussed-over looking haircuts. Everyone on the car is holding a Champagne flute. Their smiling faces reveal the preternaturally white teeth of the privileged. Waiters and waitresses in black and white circulate among the passengers offering them *hors d'oeuvres* from silver platters and fresh Champagne. Now fascinated, the driver accelerates to keep up with the monorail but as he does so he is surprised and embarrassed. Someone in the train car has noticed him looking and is now staring back at his eyes. It takes him a moment but then he realizes that he recognizes the face. It is himself.

⅋

"*Amuse-Bouche*, sir?" a voice asks from his right. A comely blond waitress with lush eye makeup is offering him "Beggars' Purses" skewered with toothpicks with little party hats from a silver platter. As she makes her offering, she looks directly into his eyes and smiles. He notices that a bit of red lipstick has made its way onto her teeth. He politely waves her off because he is engrossed in the automobile driving along the desert highway keeping pace with the monorail car in which he finds himself riding. The driver in the aging car is himself he realizes. The long shadows of the train's support beams cross the road and swipe across the auto but will cease in a moment as the sun goes below the horizon.

He scans the train's compartment. Small groups of riders are mingling. They form cells that swell then contract as they move from one to the other clutching the wine from the *Balthazar* (the label of which he now can read: Taittinger). In addition to the fact that everyone, including himself, appears well-attired and coiffed, some wear the stereotypical garb of their native countries: an Arab in a thobe, a cowboy with a western-cut dress suit sporting a 10-gallon hat and boots, an Englishman in a chalkstripe suit, with a bowler hat complete with an umbrella dangling from his forearm. It reminds him of the set of a Sixties situation comedy—perhaps the *Beverly Hillbillies.*

He turns his attention back to the car on the highway and once again locks eyes with the motorist. For an instant he sees two versions of himself—the driver of the car with his world-weary expression—and his own reflection. The car is falling behind, but then the steering wheel is in his hands as his wife and children doze tethered to their seats.

&

The monorail picks up speed and begins to rumble away into the gathering darkness. It grows quiet without the train and the only sound is the hum of the tires on the pavement. As he watches the road ahead, he thirsts for Champagne and worries about that left rear tire.

*Me, Geno and Jimmy*

# CORTEGE

*Prelude:*

*Jimmy's brother Johnny died young. I wrote in "Injection Molding" about the dangers of plastic shop work of which his death is a prime example. He had been working the floor in a shop and (as I found out later) a molding machine under intense pressure had thrown off a part which hit him in the head as he made his rounds.*

⅋

**His funeral was held** at our beautiful cathedral of Saint Cecelia's. His brother, my close friend Jimmy, was with the remaining family and Geno and I went to the service— miraculously managing to arrive early enough to be seated in a pew near the back. We were wearing our church-going black suits with skinny black ties and cheap Italian pointy shoes bought at Rockdale's dubbed "Puerto Rican Fence Climbers." The Nave smelled deliciously of incense and sun shafted down through the unadorned golden-stained glass windows as they wheeled the casket on its creaking gurney up the aisle at the end of the service.

Jimmy scanned the mourners and when our eyes met, we both smiled and repressed an urge to laugh despite the sadness of the moment. It seemed so odd to be doing this. At his young age, Jimmy had already been through this drill when his mother passed away just a few years earlier

The funeral party went down the granite steps and climbed into the cars that would constitute the procession to St. Cecelia's Cemetery a few miles from the church. Once the coffin was placed into the hearse, they were off. Geno and I stood watching the hearse, flower car, limousine (for the immediate family) and a random assortment of workingmen's cars pull away and head down Mechanic Street flying little white fringed flags with the word "FUNERAL" printed on them.

We had not taken our plan to pay our respects beyond being at the church and now we stood there on the steps watching the procession recede into the distance. Without a ride, we knew we'd have to "hoof it" to the graveside service. We walked/ran down Mechanic past the triple-decker tenements, penny candy shops and pharmacies—falling behind the procession quickly.

It was a hot summer day and we sweated through our cheap suits and confining ties. I couldn't help but think about Johnny—ever the comedian—always saying, "Look alive, here comes Simard," whenever that French Hill funeral home's black hearse would drive by. Now he lay in it having his last journey on earth. That joke, even way back then, gave me a shiver. He was one of the most naturally funny people that I've ever met but a lot of his humor had that kind of edge on it. I thought about the shotgun, the army bullets, the day he dispatched his pigeons and what seemed like a hundred stories like them.

&

We followed the same route as the procession down Mechanic, right onto Viscoloid Avenue and left onto Florence

Street. It took a while, and by the time we arrived at the cemetery—panting, sweating and with our pompadours stuck to our heads—everyone, save for the gravediggers, had left.

There were two guys there—one was wearing work gloves and was leaning on a shovel regarding us thoughtfully. The other one was sitting on a front-end loader with his hands on the controls and smoking a cigar. The motor was grumbling.

We stood there awkwardly for a moment, then, without explanation, they knew why we had come and motioned us over to look into the hole in the ground that they had just dug the day before. We inched over and peered down into the grave where the coffin was already interred in its Wilbert vault. All that was left was to cover it. It must have been a quick service.

This interlude passed and the burial crew began to swing into action. There was an awkward moment when the guy with the shovel saw that we intended to stand there watching them fill the hole. With his voice drowned out by the rising growl of the front-end loader, he shook his head and made a theatrical pushing gesture with his hands that told us that we should leave.

*Coda:*

*We turned and walked away into that brilliant summer day knowing that we had our whole lives ahead of us, but of course not what was in store. Johnny, on the other hand would not be afforded the luxury of time. His history had been written.*

*May, 1962*

# THE '56

**One sunny afternoon**, of which there seem to be so many in my memory, Jimmy parked his car in front of our house on Ninth Street and blasted the horn of his father's two-toned 1956 Chevrolet. When I went to the front door I was a little perplexed because he was nowhere near old enough to be driving. Like me he was a mere 14. I went out onto the porch like a big question mark. "C'mon let's take a spin," he coaxed. I hesitated for a second but then jumped into the shotgun seat and off we went.

Apparently his father was not around that day and the idle car became too tempting to resist. We crisscrossed the grid of numbered streets that defined French Hill, he driving with confidence and me digging the ride with my elbow out of the window. It was impressive the way he could get a pinch of rubber at the intersections considering that the Chevy was a "slush-stick."

Elvis was finally out of the army and WEIM was spinning his chart hit "Good Luck Charm" on the radio. I felt like the world was finally mine.

Presley was still singing when we pulled up next to the side of Freddy's house on Eighth and Vezina. He was a talented guitarist/singer and was holding court on the cement back stairs of the family's tidy cape. By this point his disciples had expanded to include a couple of girls and he serenaded his rapt audience from his songbook from the Fifties hits: heavy on the Buddy Holly, Eddie Cochran and of course "The King" himself. I'd seen the show and knew it well. He interspersed the songs with witty commentary that always got a laugh. I should mention here that Freddy had been a huge influence on me a few years earlier.

When Jimmy screeched his dad's Chevy to a halt those kids on the steps all stared at us slack-jawed: it must have been like seeing James Dean pull up with James Dean. Not to be upstaged, Freddy questioned whether we were old enough to be driving. Jimmy answered with another expert pinch of rubber with the automatic and we were gone like a *cooooool breeze*. Good entrance, good exit—overall a ten in my estimation.

⅋

A young man's first inclination with an automobile is to make a toy of it and Jimmy drove it over to the Little League baseball field off of Twelfth Street to put it through it's paces. He drove around the outside perimeter a couple of times and then entered the infield by the dugout. He proceeded to make his way around the bases—slow at first—but then with ever-increasing speed. *First, Second, Third, HOME!* He was acting like a madman and at one point I looked out of my window and saw only the *terra firma*.

Once he tired of this he drove the beat Chevy out of the infield and headed for home. When I looked back, there were furrows all around the base lines and an umber mushroom-shaped dust cloud hovered over the whole area.

144

He drove it the few blocks back to the forlorn little craft cottage on Eighth and parked it. When we got out, we could see that the car was totally filthy. He knew he would have to wash it before his father got home and ran for the hose. But right then there was one of those "*oh no*" moments: his brother Dicky, father-surrogate and god-of-vengeance, was storming up Gordon avenue, the pockmarks in his cheeks were glowing as if from a molten core. He was laser-focused on Jimmy and blew past me as I skulked home.

⅋

*Coda:*

*I once saw a nature documentary on television about a pride of lions on the African savannah. In this program there was a territorial dispute between the lions and a pack of hyenas. It got so serious in fact that the females and young males who would normally tend to these matters, felt so threatened that they rousted the patriarch lion from his afternoon nap to deal with this new menace.*

*The huge old cat, aggravated at being awakened, drew a bead on the alpha-male hyena which now broke and ran. His leonine majesty's powerful legs—like pistons—propelled him across the savannah in a bee line towards the interloper. At one point the lion passes a zebra that freezes in bug-eyed terror. The old lion merely glances at it as it races past at it as if to say, "This is your lucky day, motherfucker." Suffice to say, it ends badly for the hyena.*

*When Dicky charged past me on Gordon Avenue that day, I knew what it must have felt like to be that Zebra.*

*Nana and Helen, 1940s*

# HUMAN CANNONBALLS

**By 1962, my poor** mother's panic attacks had begun to make the simple act of leaving the house problematic for her. It was the kind of condition that shows up early in life and worsens over time. She had a *reticence* when she was young that seemed illogical given her gifts of good looks and modest charm. Despite her humble upbringing—something she shared with many of her generation—a casual observer might look at her and conclude that she had the world in the palms-of-her-hands with her disarming smile and sparkling Irish eyes.

But something inside of her was *ill-at-ease*. Everyone seemed to write it off as shyness but it was a different animal altogether than covered by that facile diagnosis. With the 20/20 clarity of hindsight, it seems obvious that what was beginning to complicate achieving happiness in her life was probably a psychological disorder. The closest illness to what I observed was something like *Agoraphobia* (fear of the marketplace). There is an arsenal of drugs to combat such disorders in our time, and had they existed earlier she might have been spared a lot of anguish. She described it to me a feeling that the walls were closing in, difficulty in breathing and a desire to flee. It must have been frustrating to feel like you are drowning only to have those around you stare blank-faced. It was also embarrassing for her, I'm sure.

This situation, coupled with the lack of a family car, made a long trip to the seashore unlikely but that year we managed a vacation together—my mother and I. How we got to Nantasket Beach from the landlocked Plastic City is lost to memory, but my best assumption is that one of her brothers, Edward or Robert, had driven us there. The highways of the time made that a long haul. I had rarely been to the beach, but I think it was on this journey that the sea crept into my DNA and has been calling to me ever since.

We had our picture taken on the boardwalk by a street photographer with a Polaroid camera, something I'd never seen before. When he pulled the print out, he swiped it with a chemical stick to preserve the image, and then sold it to my mother with the instruction to let it dry a little. I bought some silly souvenirs to take home and display in my room, sealing my new identity as a "Man-of-the-Sea" and she bought some postcards that wouldn't get to anyone until we were already home.

We had a room on the second floor of a rooming house/hotel close to the beach and next to Paragon Park. The room was airy and pleasant and the fragrant saline scent of the ocean permeated it. When I tired of sitting in the room, Ma gave me some money to spend to go exploring while she stayed in the cool room watching a black and white television. The curtains were billowing in the breeze when I left.

&

In the late afternoon there was a live show in the park. A poster billed it as the *Human Cannonballs* and it was about to begin. I'd seen some acts like this on TV but none had a "cannon" as huge as this one. The act was performed by the Flying…somethings with an Italian name that ended in a vowel. Logically I knew that they could not be fired from a cannon because the blast would blow them into steak-tips, but I wanted to see how they created the illusion.

After a rousing build-up by the announcer, the *Human Cannonballs*, a man and a woman dressed in pastel trapeze costumes, climbed up the top on the cannon's barrel, waving as they went. At the end they both slipped into the bore. The announcer counted it down: *10…9…8…*, and the suspense built with each descending digit. On zero there was a blast up near the tip of the barrel that echoed off of the park buildings and rattled their windows. A smoke cloud appeared followed by the daredevils' ejection from the cannon. They held hands as they hurtled through space flopping around like Raggedy Ann and Andy dolls. The net to catch them was enormous and they let go of each other just before landing in it, only to leap to their slippered feet and bound athletically down the taut web to both safety and the resounding acclaim of the crowd. It was pretty plain to me that the "cannon" was actually a catapult but I enjoyed the stunt and applauded enthusiastically along with the throng.

&

Outside Paragon Park along the cotton candy-scented sidewalk stood an assortment of food vendor booths and classic carnival games like the milk bottle knock down and the B.B. gun duck shoot with their prominent displays of potential prizes, mostly leaning towards the stuffed animal variety. The one that tickled my fancy was the ring toss game. The target area had three shelves with objects of desire attached to upright wooden dowels supported by a base of wood.

A couple of people were tossing rings when I laid down my cash for six. I had quickly locked onto my prize-of-choice; an ornate German beer stein. Now: why steins seemed so valuable to me I can't readily explain, but I'd seen some big elaborate ones at my Aunt Trudy's and the way she had them displayed made them...*special*; like trophies. I started flinging. Some of the rings did not hoop the stein, some even almost got other prizes, and couple got nothing. I could now see that the catch was the ring needed to encircle not just the prize alone, but the support block as well. This was explained to me by the vendor after I'd expended my first six rings. He then proceeded to push the ring with his stick so that it fell over the block—just to show that it could be done—although it looked to me like a pretty tight fit. I put down the last of my money for another six throws but still had no luck. With a shrug, I turned and made my way back to the room, trying to show my good sport face.

For supper we were eating Italian submarine sandwiches that my mother referred to as "heroes" when I heard the announcer pipe up, garbled as it was, from inside Paragon Park and I knew that the *Human Cannonballs* were going to do their last show of the day. I moved over to the window and peered at the park to try to see something. It was dusk by then and the lights were on inside the park. This time I knew what to expect: the countdown, the blast, the smoke and then Raggedy Ann and Andy. The puff of smoke was pastel from the three-colored spotlights as were the acrobats when they flew through the air. All I could see from this vantage point was the smoke and then their bodies going up and coming down like toast from a pop-up toaster. The muted roar from inside the walls assured me that they had survived yet again.

Although it was getting late, my stein was still calling to me and I asked my mother for a little more money to go back for one last try. It was still twilight but darkening rapidly, and the beach people were largely gone. Some of the concession stands were shuttered but I could see down the boardwalk that the Ring Toss was still open and I quickened my step. The concessioner seemed to be packing something into a corrugated box but glanced up slightly annoyed when I appeared. He looked at his watch somewhat impatiently but still sold me another half-dozen hoops.

I tossed again, but still could not get the hoop around the prize *and* the block. Once again I hit a couple of targets that I was not even aiming for. When I signaled for another set of rings the guy came over and said, "Kid, what are trying to get?" I pointed at the stein and then with his stick he pushed the ring over the block. He reached over and got an identical stein that was still in a box and handed it to me with a, "There you go." I took my *holy grail* and made my way back up the boardwalk to the room as the vendor quickly dropped the shutter of his booth and killed the light.

When I passed the main entrance of Paragon Park it was dark and there was a gate in place blocking the way in. The sidewalk was empty and all was quiet. I climbed the stairs anxious to show my prize to my mother, who waited, smoking and staying as calm as possible. I wonder whatever became of it.

*Coda:*

*I'd like to dedicate this memory to anyone who has suffered from panic attacks, especially for those who were assured that they were merely shy or misdiagnosed in some other way. I'd also like to give a shout-out to people who devote their energies to utterly meaningless causes. You know who you are.*

*Johnny Tata*

# THE WHITE GHOST

**...was what I dreamed** about being the Halloween of my seventh year. In the Fifties the costumes were usually improvised affairs; heavy on the clowns, cowboys and hobos. The latter was probably the easiest—just your father's old clothes and a five-o'clock shadow applied with a charred cork would do. But this year my mind was made up; I would be a character of my own creation: a mysterious, semi-supernatural superhero called the *"White Ghost."*

I was doodling him in school all through that October, although it wasn't really *him*, it was me. Think, if you will, of Batman, but instead of black and grey, my character would be all in white. My mind's-eye envisioned him/me swinging from one "Tarzan" swing to the next all the way down Spruce Street, on *All Hallows*. The chiseled physique, the washboard stomach, he would be magnificent. I would need the costume bespoke just for me and I called upon my mother to aid me in my quest.

Ma was not a seamstress by any means, but she knew her way around Nana's old sewing machine (the same one on which my grandmother had made all of her children's clothing) so with the big night fast approaching, she got to work.

The fabric would be of old white cotton sheets on which she had me lay down on the kitchen floor and drew around my body with a crayon to create the pattern. She then cut that in duplicate and sewed the halves together. The headpiece was separate and she cut holes for the eyes and mouth. It was early in the evening of that Halloween and the goblins and spirits were just beginning to stir when I tried my costume on for the first time.

When I went over to the mirror I was crestfallen. The reflection did not match my vision, to put it kindly. When I turned around I was kind of glad that my mother couldn't see my face because I was afraid that it would have made her sad to see my disappointment. She was kind of chuckling and reassuring me but I'm sure my body language was telling her the truth. To give this big pillowcase a shape, she cut a length of clothesline, made a belt of it and cinched it at the waist.

My entourage was knocking at the front door and it was time for the "White Ghost" to go and save the world—or whatever. My mother put some candy into the bags of the bums, clowns and cowboys and off we all went into the night. I was the smallest trick-or-treater in the posse.

&

The first house we went to was on Gordon Avenue, across the street from Jimmy's. We knocked on the storm door, stood back, and said our "Trick-or-Treat." When the lady of the house answered, she propped open the door and played *Guess the Costume* which a lot of people seem to like to do—sort of a pocket critique, if you will. She was getting them all until she got to mine. Her face screwed up into a mask of befuddlement, but then brightened as if she'd had an epiphany. She would get that one-hundred percent after all. "Oh look" she cooed sweetly beaming down at me all motherly with her hands on her knees, *"it's a little snowman!"*

&

*And then it rained.*

*Jimmy monkeying around*

# JUNK

**If you could get permission** from your parents to pitch a tent in the backyard, you opened a portal into the night. After all the lights were out in all the houses the streets were yours. Jimmy, his brother Johnny and I, liberated from our daylit lives, went off to explore this surreal version of our French Hill neighborhood.

Cote's garage and junkyard sat at the top of the hill where Ninth intersects Water and where the F&L buses hang a left for the final leg of the trip back to downtown PC via the East Side Loop. That junkyard was always beckoning our barely teenaged souls with its collection of damaged Fifties cars all alluringly cloistered behind high wooden fences on either side of the street like so many sequestered Saudi Arabian virgins.

The newest and least junky cars were in the lot nearest to the garage. We fully intended to hop over that fence to check it out but as we started trying to climb up—bumbling all over each other—late that starlit night, we heard an alarming snarl from the other side: the proverbial *Junkyard Dog* on guard duty. He sounded like a big bastard too so we abandoned that idea and moved on to plan B: the lot across the street.

We rapped on the fence a couple of times to make sure there wasn't a mutt in that lot too but there was no sound except for the first animal grumbling questions from across the street. A light went on in a house and we froze until it went dark again. We landed on our feet inside the yard and looked around; our eyes adjusting to the dim light. What were at first merely dark shapes began to grow defined in the pale glow of the stars. We padded around like Indian scouts being careful not to wake the neighbors and nervous as cats. There was no intention to do anything but look around.

We sat in few of the cars and played the radios if there was a little juice left in their batteries. There was even a bus with working lights and we had about as much fun as we could with it while trying not to make noise. Johnny sat in the driver's seat like Ralph Kramden while his brother and I played drunk passengers. He hit the horn once which caused more lights to go in the neighborhood and although he acted like it was by accident, I was not convinced.

After we exhausted all opportunities for mischief with the vehicles, we raided somebody's tomato garden on the way back to my yard and spent most of the rest of the night eating them with salt and watching for shooting stars.

&

*Interlude:*

*In those times—and in that place—the light pollution that we now take for granted barely existed, so the heavens seemed festooned with stars. In the wee hours of that summer evening, the sky bustled with activity. Some heavenly bodies seemed to move laterally above us, while others zipped through the night, their fizzling and sputtering rendered audible by the profound quiescence of the hour. It seemed the longer we looked the more we saw—and truth be known—we had begun to scare ourselves.*

*The last straw came when a flaming object roared in from the east at a low altitude. When it passed over my backyard bathing it in firelight, we actually hit the deck. Its yellow and red flames made a heavy flapping sound like flags in a stiff wind. The only observation I could make of its size was that it appeared to be half the width of our roof when it passed it over. By its trajectory, I was convinced that it was going to hit nearby and waited for the sound of an impact—but one never came. With that we decamped and retreated to our respective domiciles to pull the covers over our heads.*

☙

But Cote's also had a third lot for the junkiest of the junks—an annex of sorts—and at some point during that summer Jimmy and I hiked over to check it out. It was off of a street that no longer exists having been cut off and killed by the new I-90. It was at the foot of Rice Hill near the Johnny Appleseed birthplace marker. The short driveway through the trees opened onto a panorama of what seemed to be hundreds of Fifties autos mostly painted from the pastel palette of the era. There was no office and no adults. These babies were ours for the afternoon.

Now: what I'm going to describe is going to sound like so much vandalistic behavior, but in my own defense, I really thought of this as being a trash pile—things thrown away and therefore up for grabs, like at the city dump. That being said; it should be noted that one of the most gratifying sensations on earth must be that of a car roof caving in under your feet. The feeling of power over that symbol of adult authority was intoxicating.

We found a wrecked Studebaker with juice in the battery and fired up the radio, then thanked the car by giving it a complete makeover—a roof and hood stomping, alterations to the interior fabrics and a window treatment. *How* satisfyingly the safety glass exploded into a sparking spray of diamonds!

Having remodeled that old Stoodie about as much as was possible we moved on to a nearby Rambler (the Studebaker's still functioning radio continued to grace us with a soundtrack for this our sport). As I was bouncing on the hood and talking to Jimmy, he enlightened me to the fact that these cars were still being picked over for parts and actually *did* have monetary value. I was digesting this information while Jimmy stood on the roof with a boulder preparing to drop it through the windshield when something caught his attention behind me.

I swung around to see a police cruiser coming slowly up the drive of the lot. When I turned back to him in alarm, there was nothing but the boulder on its way to the windshield. Jimmy had disappeared. To the sound of the breaking glass, I too bolted in the direction that I thought he'd gone.

I caught up to him on the far side of the lot. We were panting and sweating when we peered around a car to see what the cops were up to. Rather than coming after us they were parked next to the Rambler. We needed to get out of there but as we cobbled together an escape plan in whispers, we realized that we couldn't walk up Mechanic Street as we had come because they could easily see us and pick us up. We felt like cornered rabbits. We'd have to go up the ridge on the other side of the lot, cut through the woods and from there make for home. This however would mean that we would have to cross the Nashua River.

When we got to the high ground we watched with fascination as the cruiser circled the lot looking for us. It struck us as kind of funny but we stopped laughing when we had to drop and freeze—another cruiser was up there on the ridge and the cop was watching the lot with binoculars. He didn't see us though and we scurried in back of the car though the brambles close enough to hear its engine still clicking.

The river was wide and swift at this point and it was hard to gauge its depth because of the pollution. It was its usual milky grey and reeked to high heaven. You didn't want to drown, especially in that water which you didn't even want to touch, but there seemed to be no better alternative. There was a fallen birch tree laying across that didn't look very substantial but it was all that there was so we would have to give it shot—Jimmy first. He yelled encouragement from the far bank as I made my way uncertainly across. My sneakers were getting wet and the tree bobbed, but held. We both looked once back at where we'd been and then headed home through the floodplain, past the foot of the dump, the filter beds and up the valley wall.

*French Hill.*

*Geno at Doyle Field*

# EGG NACHT

**It was the night before** the big high school game of the year: Leominster (Plastic) versus Fitchburg (Paper). These neighboring cities had been football rivals since the late 19th century and the Thanksgiving game was a huge event between the "Twin Cities." Leominster always seemed to be the runt of that brotherhood with its smaller population and industrial base, but in this rivalry it gave as good as it got.

On this crisp fall evening Zeke, Andy and I were sampling magazines that we knew we would never buy from the rack in Soave's Market on Seventh and Mechanic when a bunch of kids that we didn't know burst in excitedly and picked up a few dozen eggs. It was odd enough to see anyone buy eggs at that hour to catch our attention.

From what we gathered from their conversation with the owner, Fitchburg teens in cars were driving sorties through Monument Square and tossing eggs and invectives at anyone they saw downtown. I noticed as they left that they had egg yolks and shell fragments on their clothes. *DAMN: there was a war going on and we were missing it!*

We pooled our resources and bought all of the eggs the store had left in the cooler. The bemused proprietor commented on his good fortune as we settled up. Eggs were a hot commodity that November Wednesday in the Plastic City.

So armed we marched up Mechanic Street and thus unto the breach. We'd no sooner gotten to Main Street in the square when an egg whizzed by my ear and splattered against the plate glass window of Charlie's Kitchen. A shirtless kid was leaning *way* out of the passing car giving us the finger and calling us every name in the book. The car was decorated with crepe paper streamers of red and grey—Fitchburg's colors as opposed to Leominster's blue and white. We fumbled with some eggs and got off a couple of lobs that missed.

Now our attention was turned to action on the far side of the street as another streamer-covered car provoked a growing and increasingly agitated crowd in front of Monument Square at the bus stop. After completing its mission, the early-Fifties model Ford circled the war memorial monument. It would have to pass us as it made its way back to Fitchburg (or another run at the town square which was what I suspected). We would be ready this time. As they approached laying on the horn they rolled up the windows and pulled in their arms, probably out of ammo. The windows and most of the car were covered with egg yolks that dribbled over the FHS that was whitewashed on the doors. They were lucky enough to make it through that light, wisely not stopping for the yellow, but were going slow enough that we were able to score several hits at will—a satisfying splat with each one.

What had now become a howling mob, Rats and Lunchies alike, surged in the direction of our common foe and broke into a frenzied run up the sidewalks in front of the still-illuminated downtown storefronts—their mannequins feigning indifference from within.

The Ford was not so lucky at the next traffic light and was stopped behind another car waiting for the cycle to change. The driver, in his panic, stalled the vehicle repeatedly until he couldn't start it again. It was a sitting duck. Everyone now unleashed a volley on the car that was already a gooey mess. The FHS lettering was running down the doors and the crepe paper war colors were plastered to its surface.

Guys were now yanking at the locked doors furiously trying to get at the occupants as the car rocked on its suspension. In a frustrated fury they kicked the doors until they stove-in and then punched at the windows—first with their fists and then with their elbows—until holes opened. Everybody now aimed for the holes. The front echelon of the mob now scraped the broken eggs in through the breaches as the silhouettes of the four occupants huddled together in terror. Somebody climbed onto the roof and got in a few good stomps before slipping off of the yolk-drenched surface and going down hard on the gutter.

There was a pause for a moment as if the mob needed to reflect upon how far to take this thing when Geno sprang out of a downtown alley fully in the spirit of the occasion. He ran around the car once or twice gathering an egg-soaked gob of crepe paper and then thrusting it theatrically over his head like Perseus victoriously displaying the severed head of Medusa. The mob raised its arms as one and roared with pagan delight. He then stuffed this mass into a broken window just as the LPD arrived on the scene and everybody "beat feet."

⅋

*Coda:*

*And so let it be written that Geno tooketh the fall. The witnesses who were questioned (those of whom would talk) could only name one name: his. One price of local fame is that everybody knows you, and everybody seemed to know Geno. His father Joe (Italio), worked for the Leominster Police in a support role and as a special-detail officer. It was an embarrassment therefore to have his son hauled in. Geno was laying on a cell bunk at the station when Joe walked over from his nearby house to bust him loose. The son began explaining immediately that he had done nothing wrong. The father listened to the story impassively until his son had finished, but once he had, Joe had only one comment, "When you get out of here, you're getting a haircut."*

*I don't believe I went to the game that year—it would have been an anti-climax anyway.*

*Formal portrait*

# MY RED ROOM

**My mother had asked me** what color I wanted my room painted and I had decided on red—so a flat, muted shade of the color it was painted—walls and woodwork alike. It was in that room, one night, long ago that I had an uninvited visitor.

The sense of its presence woke me up and I looked out from under my covers to see it standing over me. It stooped slightly over the bed and by the position of its head it appeared to be looking back at me. It was hard to be sure though because I could discern no recognizable features. It seemed like a shadow but appeared to be three-dimensional, like someone covered with a black leotard from head-to-toe. Neither a tuft of hair on the smooth oval head nor a ripple of fabric gave me a reference point with which to identify it as human.

Our house on Ninth Street should have been inhabited as was normal on this school night: just the three of us—my parents and me. They were in the darkened parlor. Cigarette smoke and sporadic bursts of canned laughter wafted through the room's open door.

They were watching their comedies so although it was dark, I knew that it was still early enough for prime time television. I didn't need to see them to know that my mother would be sitting on her old couch at the far end of the room (the *good* couch was saved for the company that never came), and my father would be on his recliner next to a freestanding ashtray overflowing with butts. I could visualize their faces being illuminated by the flickering grayscale glow of the screen.

My room was adjacent to the kitchen where a ceiling fixture had been left on and light spilled into my bedroom through the partially open door. The silhouette continued to monitor me, moving just enough to let me know that it was alive… albeit in its own special way. Its manner was that of someone trying to make choices from a buffet table. There was no other light in bedroom, nothing to cast it into shadow. If anything it should have been illuminated by the light from the kitchen.

I didn't experience fear *per se*—I knew that my mother and father were right there after all—but I felt unable to speak or move. I could only stare back at this thing's featureless face, frozen, until finally drifting into slumber.

Although no evil had befallen me, that feeling of helpless paralysis was troubling. In the morning I casually asked my mother if anyone had come over but was not surprised when she had shaken her head and said no. This was not that kind of visitor.

Not long after what I came to call "The Black Man" incident, there was another inexplicable visitation to my Red Room (I know that there were a total of three such experiences but one has been lost to memory). We had rearranged the room so that now my headboard was up against the wall farthest from the kitchen.

This event happened later in the evening than the first, after everyone had gone to bed and the house stood in soundless darkness, but—once again—there was *someone there*. I could only faintly discern its shape, but this time something brushed my cheek. I had sprung to my feet to defend myself, not willing to be rendered helpless as before. I thrashed around in the dark room, yelling and knocking things off of my student desk and bureau—even my little TV went flying.

The ceiling light came on in the room and I saw my mother standing at its switch against a red background. The ruckus had awakened her and she wore a look of confusion, concern and... *anger?* In the light I could see my three visitors floating in the direction of the lowered venetian blinds of my window. They were small, plump and grey in color—a little like Casper the Ghost—kind of bobbing along unhurried. They had turned from me and were hovering toward, and then through the blinds, causing nary a ripple. I leapt at the last one as it went through, howling and clawing...trying to get at it. I had turned to my mother gasping for breath—my face full of questions—but if she'd seen them, she didn't then, or ever, acknowledge it.

&

*Coda:*

*The obvious explanation for these encounters is that I was in some kind of dream state. At the time I thought these were isolated events peculiar to me. But as I have come to find out, they have the earmarks of similar occurrences common to many. I have read of them being called "Waking Dreams" or "Sleep Paralysis," but I would wager that the majority of victims of these phenomena—myself included—**know** that these events are **not** all in one's head.*

*Geno and Ray*

# NATURE'S WAY

**My first job was in** the summer of 1965 when I was about to enter my senior year at Leominster High School. My running-buddy, Geno, was taking Culinary Arts at Saxon Trade and through that and a connection with the Holiday Inn management, he had landed a job as an apprentice chef.

The sparkling modern hotel stood on a site next to busy Routes 2 and 12, the main roads to Fitchburg and not far from the huge Foster Grant factory.

Geno told me that they had an opening for a dishwasher that summer and that I should apply, and with his recommendation I got the job. I would be happy to earn a little money that summer, but I was living with my parents and could go without it. Geno on the other hand, at age 16, had a wife and a new baby, so his position was more critical. One of Geno's enticements for me to take the job was the chance to see movie star Jayne Mansfield who'd be staying at the Inn in July. *Sold!*

The head chef was the boss, and on my first day, he gave me a tour of the kitchen and a rundown of my responsibilities, which went like this: The busboys would drop off trays of dirty dishes and silverware at the beginning of what in effect was a production line. I needed to grab them, scrape the garbage into the disposal, rinse them, put them on a rack and push them into an industrial strength dishwasher. Every so often I would pull the racks of now clean and steaming dishes over and stack them onto shelves where they would dry and cool off. Soon a new cycle would begin with them being refilled with new orders and served up to another sitting of hungry customers.

The chef was from Germany and spoke with a thick accent. He had sparse close-cropped, lead-colored hair, and projected an air of authority. He was obviously not accustomed to being fucked with. When he would come over to yell at us about something, we would raise our left forefingers up to our upper lips for moustaches, click our heels and give *"Heil Hitler"* salutes with our right arms, throwing in a couple of goose steps for good measure. This was once he turned his back of course. The *Kitchen Nazi* had one strict edict for the dishwasher: NO OLIVE PITS IN THE DISPOSAL! *DAS IST VERBOTEN!... NEIN!...NEIN!...NEIN.*

Dawn broke on my new job, the dishwasher's conveyer belt chugged forward and the detritus of peoples' breakfasts started coming my way. I started scraping, rinsing and getting the dishes and silverware into the washer. It was at a steady pace for breakfast and I barely kept up to it until the rush ended.

Waitresses in ridiculous Victorian maid costumes toddled in and out though the swinging doors, to and from the chintzy red world of the dining room into the steamy grease-smelling brushed-aluminum atmosphere of the kitchen. When they entered, their frozen customer smiles dissolved into expressions of resigned determination as they placed or picked up their orders, threw salads together and rubbed their feet whenever they could find time.

The pace quickened towards lunch. The waitresses were trying to hurry so much that one would occasionally fall on her duff slipping on the damp floor which seemed kind of comical until they'd burst into tears and we'd rushed to help her up. The dishes and garbage piled up as I fell behind. The dishwashing machine was boiling hot in the un-air-conditioned kitchen and I ran with sweat trying to keep up. I kept thinking of Lucy and Ethel in the episode where they worked for a chocolate factory.

In order to survive, I was going to have to disregard the *Kitchen Nazi's* rule regarding olive pits because separating them slowed me down too much. I started to dump them into the disposal with the rest of the garbage. They started popping back out of the disposal and fusillading the kitchen with shrapnel almost immediately. *Beoww...beoww.* I glanced over at the chef's desk where he was working to see if he noticed. He was looking around like he was trying to figure out what was happening and I kept hoping that he wouldn't.

&

One of Geno's and my tasks was to clean up the kitchen at the end of the work day once everybody else had punched out. We fat-mopped the linoleum as fast as we could then made our way over to the most golden perk of the job: the hot fudge warmer. If you have ever had a hot fudge sundae, you have probably had the experience of spooning out the bottom of the goblet with that long spoon and wishing that there was more. With nobody watching, we created huge sundaes, gorged ourselves, and went back for more. After a week or so the chef was wondering why he already had to order new hot fudge and questioned us about it to which we just shrugged our fattening shoulders.

&

As promised Jayne Mansfield arrived in July. The blond bombshell was referred to derisively as "the poor man's Marylyn Monroe" and if M.M. was a self-created caricature of

the stereotypical sexy dumb blond, Mansfield was a caricature
of that caricature. It didn't matter to us, Hollywood glamour
was coming to the Plastic City and we were in the front row
for the show.

She was in town to do a week of summer stock strutting
her considerable stuff on the boards of the Whalom playhouse
in a flimsy farce called *Nature's Way*. She arrived at the Inn in
a van that was used to promote a product that she endorsed; a
mattress (subtle), and her likeness and name were plastered all
over the truck. After the chef shit-canned me, Geno still tried
to sneak me in to the hotel to get a peek at her, but never with
any success.

Geno on the other hand actually got to meet her while
bringing lunch for the star, her family and entourage. Her son
"Zot" was an intolerable nuisance and Geno had the task of
keeping the brat out of trouble. The actress had taken a liking
to Geno and he became a kind of unofficial liaison between the
Inn and the starlet, probably because the management wasn't
quite sure how to handle such an exotic creature. What all this
had to do with Culinary Arts is a mystery. He started taking a
few of his breaks with the party where she held court by the
pool.

That July the place took on a magic-realism quality as if
the Hollywood pixie dust had transformed the Plastic City's
most modern hotel pool into a David Hockney painting. Geno
lifted weights in those days and Mansfield was noted for her
fondness for musclemen, such as her second husband and
former Mr. Universe, Micky Hargitay. Geno and she did some
friendly frolicking in the pool which included her riding on his
shoulders in her famous leopard-print bikini.

The Holiday Inn management was monitoring all of this
with jaundiced eyes and soon decided that Geno was having a
little too much fun to be on the payroll, so by mutual agreement
he moved on.

And with that the episode closed, but that July in 1965, the radiance of Jayne Mansfield's star power transformed the PC from the black and white Fifties into the Technicolor Sixties. That was her gift to our adolescence.

⅋

The day I reported to work when the Kitchen Nazi fired me he explained the reason to me even though I didn't ask. Working in the position that I had only recently occupied an old man was darting around. We are talking late-seventies, I'm not kidding. "You see that guy? At his age he moves twice as fast as you do," said the chef. I'd have to admit the geezer was really hauling ass. I took my last check and walked out into the summer sunshine. I did not bother to Nazi salute when I left. In my mind it's one of those crane shots where the camera pulls away just before they roll the credits of my movie. *The End.*

Geno never became a chef which is a shame because in this day of celebrity chefs, he would have been a natural. He is no stranger to television and has a program on local cable (LATV) in the Plastic City called *The World According to Geno*. Today where the Holiday Inn once stood now stands a nursing home. How apropos of the passage of time, wouldn't you agree?

⅋

*Coda:*

*Jayne Mansfield's once-promising movie career had fizzled and she took a nightclub act on the road. In June 1967 that road had brought her to Biloxi, Mississippi for a gig at a supper club. The following morning she had a publicity interview on a New Orleans television program and she and her current boyfriend, a driver and three of her children jumped into their Buick Electra 225 to begin the trip. They stopped along the way to be feted by some friends and then hopped back onto U.S. Highway 90 bound for the Big Easy with the road to themselves and a license-to-fly. At 2:25 a.m. they came upon a tractor-trailer that had virtually stopped for a truck that was spraying a mosquito fogger. With no time to brake, the Buick screeched into the back of the trailer and under it, shearing off the top of car and killing the three adults*

175

*riding up front. Fortunately her children who had been sleeping in the back seat received only minor injuries. The gruesome detail of the accident is that Jayne Mansfield's famously beautiful head had been severed, but there is some conjecture as to whether or not this is an urban myth.*

*What is not conjectural is that she was only 34-years-old. In the wake of this high-profile accident the National Highway Traffic Safety Administration (NHTSA) began requiring that an "underside guard of strong steel tubing" be attached on all tractor-trailers to prevent just such an accident. Its nickname is a "Mansfield Bar." The next time you come up behind a trailer truck you will notice it if you look for it. That's another gift Jayne left us.*

*Portsmouth Harbor*

# WHITE NOISE

**The woman who sat across** the linen-covered table from him in a Boston restaurant was not his wife. She was in fact wife of another man and the best friend of his own estranged spouse. They each sipped from their first glasses of a wine not worthy of its price tag while trying to select from their menus all the while struggling to maintain an appropriate amount of awkward small talk. He'd known her for as long as he'd known his wife, from the giddy early days when she had introduced him to all of her best friends. But they had rarely seen each other over the course of the seven-year union.

She had called him at his job at an architect's office in Cambridge to initiate this meeting which had evolved into this *tête-à-tête*. He surmised that it was going to be about possibly brokering a *rapprochement* between his ex-wife and himself. Although still somewhat shaken by the separation, he had mixed feelings about starting over, if that in fact was what was to be laid on the table. Nonetheless he would hear her out.

That table was near a large fountain that looked something like the snow-covered Matterhorn. Water gushed down a shoot from the top and worked its way to the base over a tortuous course. It was strategically placed to provide a visual focal point for the room as well as white noise to mute the diners' conversations and provide a sense of privacy (and intimacy). The cavernous restaurant murmured, gurgled and echoed with its indecipherable phase-shifted hum punctuated intermittently by the clack/rattle of silverware and china. Their waiter walking away with their orders scribbled on his pad was the signal to cut-to-the-chase. He looked at her pleasantly but quizzically and waited for her to commence. As if taking the cue she started, "I'm worried about you." It took him aback because he barely knew her really and couldn't imagine what she would be worried about.

He chuckled hoping to sound reassuring and said, "I just need to figure out how to cook something, do my own laundry and pay the bills."

"No...I know...it's not that," she responded, "I had a dream about you trying to kill yourself."

"I'm not *that* bad off," he reassured her, somewhat embarrassed but asked when the dream had taken place.

"Last spring...you were hanging off of a cliff...or something," she answered with an expression that hoped she'd rung a bell.

He cast his memory back to the previous spring. He was no rock climber; strictly a sea-level dweller whose ears popped at 25 feet and during that time he and his wife had been living in Portsmouth, New Hampshire—a long way from the mountains.

Although that had been a low point in his life emotionally due mainly to their flagging marriage, dim financial prospects and the recent loss of his mother—he was never suicidal and hoped never to be. As he searched his memories however, an incident began to trickle in through the cracks in time. He hadn't thought of it since then but now it flooded the hold of his mind and made him wonder if this had been what the woman had viewed in her prophetic dream—one that had been real enough for her to bring them together. As he began to think about that spring day, the echoing gurgle of the room filled his ears as his eyes turned inward.

&

He'd had the impulse to run that morning—but as always—there was nowhere to go. Their hard-partying ways, once so exciting, had begun to turn ugly and words and deeds between them made their union seem like a lost cause.

It had been one of *those* Friday nights and he'd awakened to her turned back but knew that, though she feigned sleep, was in fact awake. Rather than face her, he had dressed and headed out onto the sidewalk on Market Street in the direction of Strawbery Banke. Their apartment was in one of the old brick warehouse buildings that had been converted to living space and boasted a nice view of the river, tugboats and river traffic from the back window above Ceres Street.

He had no particular destination: just...*elsewhere*—a familiar journey indeed. This flight took him past "The Banke" and out onto Peirce Island. He passed the public swimming pool and traced the southern edge of the island with the intention of circumnavigating it. This eventually brought him to the chain-link fence that surrounded the water treatment facility. He was still able to continue on a path to the outside of the fence until he came to an *impasse;* a chasm cut a hole in the path behind the treatment plant. He'd had a single-minded determination to keep going but now he was forced to reassess his plan.

He figured he was halfway around the island and now stood on a 60-foot bluff that overlooked the Piscataqua River—wide at this point—with Kittery, Maine in the distance. The cleft blocking his progress was some 40-feet-wide. It had been created over eons by an underground stream flowing into the river along with erosion from the river currents and tidal movements. He inched over and craned his neck to look down at it and small pebbles fell into the hole.

When they'd installed the fence around the plant, they'd rolled it out but merely strung it loose across this stretch without some of the poles that should have supported it due to the absence of ground to drive them into. Here the aluminum mesh hung a bit loosely and shimmied and jingled slightly in the wind off the water.

This was not the first chain-link fence that he'd encountered in his days. He was 30 at this time and still in possession of most of the strength of his youth, or so he thought, so on impulse, he decided to go for it. He jumped out onto the fence and clawed his fingers into the mesh, and with the toes of his sneakers doing their best to gain purchase under him, hand-over-handed his way across the expanse. Halfway in he knew that he'd made a mistake. The loose fence squealed and sagged startlingly with the addition of his weight and it both swayed him in the wind and tilted him at a severe angle toward the river. He looked down at the pit of the chasm considering his chances should he fall...and they were not promising.

Now in his heightened mental state, the arrangement of rocks and soil inside the fissure seemed to assume the countenance of an evil and ugly beast eager to feed and both surprised and delighted by its good fortune. The din of natural sounds seemed to combine to form words. *"No one ever comes here...no one,"* it groan-whispered. The last people to visit this the anus of Peirce Island had probably been the fence builders themselves and they had no doubt finished as fast as they could and scurried off happy to be gone from this shunned place— especially if they'd seen the face too—*or heard its voice.*

A gull glided over and looked into his eyes noncommittally curious. It was able to kite on an updraft and seemed scarcely to move out of a four-foot-square quadrant of space all the while regarding his face. It too, seemed to caw, *"No one ever comes here…no one."* It was getting harder to monkey across now with his feet no longer able to provide any support, and his blood-drained fingers ached.

Thirty was beginning to feel older by the second. He looked up at the squealing fence and wondered how long the rusty tension bands would hold the mesh to the far posts. Beneath him in the ebb and flow in the mouth of the chasm, loose rocks clacked together like racked billiard balls which with his escalated sensibility sounded like a song of merriment. "No one ever comes here…no one," they chuckled. Their chorus joined the roar of the wind, the caws of the gull and the basso profundo from the wretched black maw of the abysm itself in some *macabre* oratorio composed by a dark god especially for this special occasion entitled: **"Just…Let…Go."** He turned toward the river searching for the remote possibility of rescue but only the black windows of the abandoned naval prison in Kittery stared back—dead-eyed. **"NO ONE EVER COMES HERE…NO ONE."**

⅜

Yet somehow he made it across only to collapse exhausted. At first he sat on the chasm's far edge and then lay on his back on the thin crust of soil that covered the stony bluff and signed the cross; thankful to be alive. The possibility of what might have happened to him now began to sink in. The gull sailed over one last time to scan a shadow across his form and issue a final sarcastic squawk before gliding up into the sun. The water in the chasm still rumbled and echoed, the loose rocks clacked, the wind roared and the fence jingled, but now they'd returned to being what they were and nothing more.

He continued on the path that inevitably circled back to the troubled apartment in that old brick city hunkered down beside the deep and churning Piscataqua. Could he have died? Yes. And what a pathetic death it would have been. What would one proclaim it? Death by Misadventure? Maybe Death by Daredeviltry? *How about Death by I Don't* **Give** *a Fuck?*

Though that entire incident had streaked though his mind in detail, he only told the woman that he had been depressed at that time and had taken a foolhardy risk by climbing a chain -link fence across a gorge—a stunt dangerous enough to have killed or crippled him.

With the white noise murmuring in the background, she nodded sagely at this. Her dream had been validated. That's what she had envisioned—him dangling over an abyss. Dinner was done and they signaled for the check. She reached across the table to touch his hand meaningfully and say, "However things turn out, life is worth living…okay?" To this he just nodded.

*Coda:*

> *He had missed the last Blue Line train so she'd offered to give him a lift back to his apartment near Revere Beach. They drove mostly in silence until they got to the Victorian triple-decker on Beach Street where he now lived on his own.*

> *She stopped and put the car into Park, leaving the engine idling for the heat. As they chatted a bit more the snow began to coat the windshield sequestering them in shadows and muffling the outside sound. There was awkward silent pause—but in the end he thanked her for her concern and forced a laugh. She just seemed relieved to have the dream vindicated.*

> *He got out, crouched down as people will do to say goodnight to drivers in cars, then ski-skated through the beige snow covering the walkway up to his pad, pausing once to watch her car's tail lights recede behind hissing curtains of snow.*

*The Nile Hilton, 1988*

# EGYPT

*Prelude:*
*After three months of working for my company's operation in Jeddah, Saudi Arabia, I was eligible for a paid trip home which also included an overnight stop at a destination of my choice along the route. London was on the list, as was Casablanca, but I chose Cairo. I have always loved and been fascinated by Egyptian art and history and this was my chance to go to the source. Years earlier I had read an article by Ken Kessey about his visit to the pyramids in* Rolling Stone Magazine *that had stirred my imagination and stayed with me since. And of course you have love Boris Karloff in* The Mummy *from 1932 (Tannis anyone?).*

&

**Cairo**
   **The view from my cab** from the airport revealed a low-rise city that looked as if it would all come down come toppling down from a mild temblor. I, however, was booked into a room

on the seventh floor of the substantial Nile Hilton, overlooking the river itself. After registering I headed up to my room and while walking down a corridor couldn't help but notice a young Arabic-looking woman—nicely dressed in red—half in and half out of a room threshold. Unlike in the Kingdom of Saudi Arabia, Egypt is a liberal Moslem country and culturally the full-body black Abaya isn't mandatory. I was wearing my red *Rebel Without a Cause* windbreaker and clutching my Fender Stratocaster in its Fifties retro-tweed carrying case; so perhaps that was why she was staring at me but as I often do when being stared at, I said hello to break the tension. She returned the greeting smiling tentatively but as I walked past, I noticed a large Arabic man inside the room glowering at me bug-eyed, nostrils aflare. I confess to stepping-up my pace a little.

I had a great room with a huge marble bathroom and a balcony overlooking the Nile which was all well and good but more importantly—since I had not had a drink (nor a woman for that matter) in three months—there was a well-stocked mini-bar. *Scooby-Doo I had work to do.* I spent the afternoon catching rays, enjoying the river and exploring the mini-bar.

After a room service club sandwich I figured I would walk across the *Kasr Alniel* Bridge to see if I could find a bar on the other side of the Nile. I had learned in The Kingdom that the pace of life quickened after sunset in the Arab world once things cooled off. These were nocturnal people whose societal habits had been shaped over centuries by the heat of the sun.

Cairo proved to be no different. The under-illuminated bridge was teeming with humanity but little car traffic. I had not even gotten onto the sidewalk of the bridge before being accosted by street vendors. They were selling "ancient" Egyptian scenes printed on papyrus along with some other tourist trinkets. There was more to be seen under the bridge, a salesman informed me with a directional sweep of the arm. *Oh yeah, right.*

I began to cross the bridge and wished that I hadn't even

before I was halfway across. Between my blond hair and red jacket I might just as well have had an American flag stuck to my head. Mendicants and pitchmen converged on me from every direction. Once I got to the other side I could see that there was nothing of interest there and turned back. I had learned very little Arabic during my three months in Saudi, but I did know the word "*la*" which means no and as I retreated from the bridge I was saying it firmly, if self-consciously, every few steps.

At one point, an old man came up to me dragging a 12-year-old boy after him. He jabbered at me in Arabic—snot running out of his nose and into his hennaed goatee. He was gesturing at the boy's eyes which appeared to be blinded and pussy. Obviously he wanted money but there was no way I was flashing my wallet on that bridge, and I tried to keep moving even though he was now clutching my sleeve. I noticed three well-dressed, college-aged Egyptian boys coming my way and this little drama seemed to have caught their attention. I was wary, figuring they might start insisting that I give the beggar money or maybe even starting a fight with me. Instead one of them came up to me and said in English, "Mister, you have to *run*." That was all I needed. I didn't run but shook free and strode purposefully back to the hotel, grateful for the tip.

⅋

**Giza**

I woke up late the following morning and headed down for some breakfast. I bypassed the buffet and bellied up to the bar. Once fortified, I made my way to the hotel lobby to try to arrange transportation out to the pyramids and Sphinx. It turned out to be easy for when I went outside there was a kindly-looking Egyptian who reminded me of Anwar Sadat leaning against the fender of a vintage, mellow-yellow Mercedes. "Do you want to see the Sphinx?" he asked. His pronunciation of Sphinx sounded like *Sfink-sa*. I said yeah but asked how much. It would be $40 for the car and driver all day including a ride

*185*

to the airport the following morning. Deal made; we motored off to Giza.

The city and suburbs ended abruptly and there stood the pyramids against the backdrop of the vast Sahara. I'd seen it so many times in books and on television that I felt that I'd been there already. My driver parked and waited while I went into the Pyramid of Chephren. There was one of these deals where you had to pay some guy who looks like an official to watch your car—whatever. You buy a little ticket from him without faith because it looks like another little scam. He may or may not have been associated with the pyramid in an official capacity.

Just as Ken Kessey had written, as you approach the pyramid, because of its shape, it flattens out as you get close to it and does not appear tall at all. You have to stoop a little to go in but then down you go through a tilting shaft on which someone has built a wooden ladder of sorts to give tourists some footing. Some sweating middle-aged guy gave me an "it's-not-worth-it" look as he passed me coming out with his family as I was going down.

At the bottom of the ramp, I walked along a dust-of-ages floor and the atmosphere became very cool and pleasant. All that lit the place was a string of bare light bulbs that looked very temporary like a construction site. There was a gloom about the place that I adored—silent as a tomb (not surprising I guess).

I was there at that time quite alone. One comes to the extremely worn stone cavity of a sarcophagus that Ken Kessy had described in his article. It reminded me of a watering trough. Kessy had dropped acid before going into the pyramid, probably not a good idea, but who am *I* to judge? He had said that the sarcophagus had reeked of urine and that he had vomited at the smell of it. Well, it did not smell like that when I was there, although I had the impulse to use it for that purpose myself out of need following my liquid breakfast.

Out of respect, however, I contained myself. All I can report about the inside of the Chephren pyramid is that there are no hieroglyphics or statuary in evidence, and that the shape of the space is something that I had not experienced before or since. It's large and cavernous, cut at odd sharp angles with mysterious corridors running off in unexpected directions. It's really quite unique.

When I emerged from the tomb I was out of matches and I asked a little street-urchin if he had a light. He said that he did, but the price was one cigarette. You gotta hustle baby. Later on I was standing by the side of *Cairo-alex* Desert Road smoking the Marlboro when a string of saddle horses carrying tourists canted by. It was a beautiful sight and on instinct I swiped the flank of one of the steeds as it passed me. The tour guide on the lead horse noticed and yelled back over his shoulder that the contact would cost me one Egyptian pound. Such is commerce in the Middle East.

I split the rest of the afternoon between the Cairo Museum and souvenir shopping. The museum was big but too small for the collection that it housed. Take the best Egyptian collection you've ever seen and times it by ten and it's like that. Artifacts are stacked on top of more artifacts.

⚘

*Coda:*

*In the morning I settled-up at the front desk with my driver helping translate the transaction which was pretty pricey because someone appeared to have gotten into the mini-bar. On the way out my driver offered to show me the stadium where the real Anwar Sadat had been assassinated. I thought President Sadat was a great man and his death a tragedy but it was time to go home without delay. I'd now seen the pyramids and the Sphinx. I would have my memories, a couple of pictures and a Nile Hilton towel, "stolen fair and square" as we used to say back in the Plastic City.*

*Teddy Boys*

# OMERTA

*Prelude:*
*As the Fifties shuffled into the Sixties there was an incident that so shocked the Plastic City that five decades later an unuttered oath-of-silence precludes anyone from speaking, writing or depicting it in any way, shape, form or fashion. In its time it thrust an anonymous little shop town beside a dirty river onto the world stage, but not in a way that anyone would take pride in. The drama that unfolded is the stuff of great literature, theatre and film, but today there is scant evidence of its existence. For all intents and purposes it simply doesn't.*

**Hell-on-Wheels**

**It began with a** dozen or so young men tooling around Leominster in three matching black '52 Fords that served as their movable clubhouse one hot summer long ago. Like a marauding army they wreaked havoc as they made swaggering figure-eights around and throughout the PC. Free-living and free-swinging. They wore the fashion of the time—hair greased back into duck's asses—collars turned up and a don't-fuck-with-me attitude to match. A bunch of Brandos and Deans they were, fueling themselves on Narragansett Giant Imperial Quarts (GIQs) of beer and red-pack Pall Malls. Hell-on-wheels and a thorn under the saddle of the Leominster Police Department.

Life turns on a dime though and their joyride ended when they crossed the line from juvenile mischief to felonious malice in an impetuous criminal act that landed even the most uninvolved of them behind the bars of the roughest prisons in Massachusetts for the duration of the primes of their youths. They may have been still in their teens but they would get their stripes with the big boys.

Their shocking incident made the papers worldwide and they were so vilified back home that when they were marched into court to face their charges, State Police snipers needed to be positioned on adjacent rooftops to scan the agitated mob that had assembled for potential assassins. Threats had been made against their lives and there were some there that day who'd screamed for their heads. They were all found guilty and sentenced based upon the degree of their participation. Those with the least involvement, such as the ones who merely plotted it in Monument Square and never got into the cars, would do their time for "Conspiracy." They entered the system and began crossing the passing days off their calendars, one square at a time.

This created a paradigm shift in Leominster and after that parents began monitoring their teenagers' activities and images with a higher level of scrutiny. The goop came out of the hair, the collars went down and the leather jackets and boots went to the Catholic Charities. The Fifties were dead in the Plastic City—long may they live—and the Sixties began to chug forward. In due time, the players in this drama, having paid their debts to society, began to meander home.

❧

## The Party

I can't recall how the self-named Teddy Boys got the gig to play at Donny's surprise coming home party. We didn't have much of a band: just Ray on bass, and Zeke and I on cheap electric guitars. We'd been hacking through some folk music for a while (everyone on French Hill played guitar it seemed) but with the advent of the British Invasion, we became inspired enough to take a crack at performing for an audience with a few chestnuts like "Long Tall Sally" and "Rock My Soul." All nervous in our bellies and apprehensive about the prospect of playing our ill-rehearsed handful of hand-me-down three-chord songs in front of witnesses we lugged our raggedy-ass assortment of amplifiers and instruments up to the second floor of a three-decker tenement on West Street to set up. There would be no PA system, just the bass and guitars with us singing as loud as we could over the din. The hosts positioned us in the most logical place for a Christmas tree and, ready as we were going to be, we started twanging away.

The Teddy Boys may not have been happening that night but the party was. Donny obviously had a lot of friends who were eager to welcome him home. The hosts had given us a little spiked punch and we fumbled through our mistake-riddled repertoire leaving long spaces between songs as we sipped our drinks and stalled for time. Mercifully it didn't take long for the guests to lose interest in us and get back to socializing.

Finally, the much-anticipated moment arrived. Someone had called from a payphone to announce that the Man-of-the-Hour would soon be arriving. They shushed us and the room became electric. We all listened to the sound of echoing footfalls on the stairs and then the hall which made everybody's heart thump.

He entered to a *surprise* that could have woken the dead. There were embraces, shoulder slaps and handshakes all around and Zeke, Ray and I put down our guitars and joined the welcoming circle at its outer fringe.

The guest of honor was lovingly jostled to the center of the living room and enthroned on a wooden kitchen chair. An archtop sunburst acoustic guitar materialized and was placed into his arms like a baby to rock. "Play us a song Donny," someone requested to a chorus of approval. He plucked the strings one at a time, ear-tuning as he went. Once satisfied he launched into one called "Oh Julie." I now know that it was originally recorded by the Crescendos but that night was the first time I'd heard it. It sounded like it had been written in Heaven for Buddy Holly, one of my idols. That night however it was Donny who was crushing it.

&

It was now the Sixties and the dawn of the Beatles era which had begun while Donny was a guest of the Commonwealth, and with his James Dean horned rims, Elvis conk of dark brown hair, Buddy Holly delivery and throwback song—good as he was—he seemed like an anachronism. The world had evolved while he was on ice and there would be no buying that time back.

Not that it would have made a difference to his adoring friends. At one point, a girl who was standing in the circle turned away from his show to glare at me reproachfully and ask rhetorically, "Where's *he* been all night?" What was there to answer? She was attractive and I'd noticed her earlier so I'd have to say that one stung a little. But there was no question that she was right. He blew us out of the water.

&

*Coda:*

*Of course that night (incidentally my first gig) was never meant to belong to me. I was doing what I've done myriad times since—providing a little background/dance music—it was about Donny. But in thinking about that party, I kind of wonder if watching the way he electrified that room stayed with me all my years of performing...in search of that same fix.*

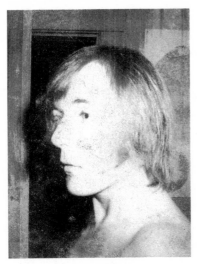

*1969*

# XIN LOI

**Following my six months** of active duty training for the National Guard, I returned to my job at the Thom McCann warehouse in Leominster. I was still trying to scrape up the tuition to the Art Institute of Boston, a feat I would not achieve until the age of 21. Some of the faces at the shop were new, but as before, I knew pretty much everybody. I'd gone to school with a lot of them so we were close in age.

It sometimes felt like we were a lost generation in a way, living in that small factory town with its low-paying jobs to compete for and the Viet Nam war hanging over our heads. This is to say nothing of the war souvenirs for the folks back home: distaste and distrust of government—and by extension—all authority...oh yeah, and drugs. A resigned hopelessness seemed to permeate the place and we felt like we were nowhere and were going nowhere. All you heard was "It don't *mean* nothin'," one of the war's sardonic catchphrases.

Thom McCann was a good gig all things considered; no

real heavy lifting and decent wages by local standards. You had to join the Teamsters to work there and although we hated paying the dues, we enjoyed the protection and the yearly raises. For a lot of us, Thom McCann was our first *real* job and our indoctrination into the "Work Ethic." We worked hard when the work was there but there was also some downtime. Many of us were imbibing on what there was to imbibe too—I mean—it *was* the Sixties after all.

&#8494;

One particular workday a bunch of us made the spontaneous decision to have lunch at the closest watering hole which was amusingly named McCann's. Their menu was mostly of the liquid variety but they did have bar staples like pickled eggs, Slim Jim's and chips. We ordered a tray full of longnecks and grabbed a table near the window where we could make fun of passersby.

Chandler plunked some coins into the jukebox and Jimi Hendrix and his Strat started wailing "Foxy Lady." Ray bought a half-dozen bags of Tri-Sum potato chips—the PC's very own brand—and splayed them on the table. He had a funny way of clapping his hands on the bags to pop them open. When I checked the clock, I was surprised to find that our lunch hour was almost over. We started finishing our beer and getting ready to get back to the warehouse when Pete appeared at the table carrying a tray of shots. We all groaned and sat back down. Ray went over and pumped more coins into the Wurlitzer and the music and the spirits became a river that we bobbed along like rubber duckys on a sunny Sunday afternoon.

&#8494;

After an indeterminate period of time the kid who was being groomed for a management position showed up on the sidewalk and peered through the window at us, shading his eyes with his hand like he was saluting. He had the balls to come in and address the table with a nasty little grin on his face. The boss had given him the dirty work of sniffing out his

*194*

wayward Teamsters and issuing them an ultimatum: *get back to work or be fired!* We'd had the good sense not to drive to the bar and now we hurriedly bumbled back up Adams Street to punch in. The boss monitored us as we did, his arms crossed over his chest. His little *protégé* was standing behind him in the same pose smiling his nasty little grin again. I grudgingly concede that round to the front office.

⅋

As we dried out for the remainder of the day, Chandler and I worked the line—checking orders and making sure that the shoes in the cartons matched the order forms before sealing the cartons and sending them down to the loading dock.

Having just done my active duty I had the Army fresh in my mind and I knew that he had recently returned from serving as an infantryman in Viet Nam, so I wanted to pick his brain about his experiences in-country. Chandler had grown his black hair out and looked a little like mid-1960s-era Paul McCartney. He had a likably goofy manner and as he told some tales about his hitch, just the sound of his voice was enough to make me laugh.

Perhaps the stories he was telling had jogged his memory but I began to notice that his mood had darkened. When the line stopped he lit a cigarette and his eyes seemed to turn inward. He emotionally blurted out that he'd killed some people in "The Nam." I respectfully philosophized that death was an inevitable consequence of combat (easy for me to say never having been to a war zone). Regaining control, he went on to elaborate.

⅋

*He had been on a patrol and his platoon had bivouacked for the night near a village. As it grew dark, his Captain ordered him to set up an M-60 machine gun behind some fallen trees that partially blocked a dirt road. Chandler asked the captain if he should issue a challenge to anyone approaching but the Captain had said no. "If they're coming from that flank they're the bad*

195

*guys...light 'em up.'' So Chandler nestled the"Pig" into position and hunkered down for the night, trying his best to stay awake.*

*Some hours later there were sounds coming from way down the road. He went from nearly dozing off to high-alert in a heartbeat. He could make out the sibilance of whispered words, some rustling and the intermittent muffled clanging of metal objects—and it was growing louder. He aimed the weapon in the direction of the sounds; his heart racing. He could see nothing in the blackness at first but as the sounds got closer he began to make out some silhouettes and opened up on them. The noise of the M-60 was deafening as it shattered the jungle's silence. The illuminated figures flickered for a moment like dancers caught in a strobe light. When he ceased fire, all he could hear was the gunfire echoing off of the hills and the ringing in his own ears. The Captain and part of the platoon had now joined him behind the blockade but no one was to go beyond that point until daybreak.*

*At dawn the platoon cautiously—weapons ready—stalked over to an assemblage of bodies littering the road. There were eight corpses in total, but they were neither Viet Cong nor North Viet Namese regulars. They were unarmed old people, women and children. The M-60's large caliber rounds had done their job all too well and even to the young soldiers' increasingly calloused eyes it was a gruesome sight to behold.*

❧

Chandler pleaded with me or perhaps himself, that there was no way that he could have known who those people were in that darkness as if I—or anyone—was there to pass judgment on him. It seemed like he was defending his soul against his conscience in a court-martial he'd convened in his own brain. I wanted to tell him that of course he could not have known that they were non-combatants and that he had only obeyed direct orders, but anything I could have said would have sounded empty and inadequate at that moment, so I just stood there. When the line started up again, breaking the silence, I felt kind of relieved to go back to sealing shoe cartons.

*With a friend in my backyard, 1950s*

# CAT'S EYE

*Prelude:*
*I've stated it in previous entries but it bears repeating: I am a total sucker for animals. Now, I know that it is a contradiction in that I'm not a vegetarian—but outside of that—I would be hard-pressed to harm one unless my life depended on it. I once won two lobsters in a game and I took them to Magnolia Beach, removed the elastics from their claws and shouting, "Run mon ami, you are free," tossed them into the waves, much to my wife's horror and dismay. Any time I have seen lobsters in a holding tank I have felt the impulse to buy them all and give them their freedom, with an admonition not to be so stupid next time. Fins, feathers, scales or fur: animals get the pass. However, I have a particular affinity for cats.*
*I've had them around me since I was little. We had a big Tom named Tata (pronounced Tah-Tah to have some fun with the pronunciation of our family name that everyone mispronounces, it*

*should be Tay-Tah). Tata once tried to pull a Thanksgiving turkey right off the kitchen table until I stopped him. I'm sure he knew he wouldn't get away with it but I guess it was just too tempting.*

*Somewhere along the line we adopted a female and there was a litter of kittens before you knew it. Everyone seemed to want one and there was no problem finding homes for them—all save one that was just too cute to part with. Soon there were two litters that came at once and everybody we knew who might have been interested in a kitten already had one. And this is how it happened ladies and gentlemen; my mother unwillingly became a "Cat Lady." People started dropping unwanted felines into our yard and things got way out of control. We eventually worked our way through this problem but there was pain attached because we loved the cats with their own little names, fur markings and personalities. Now comes the warning: **a cat will be harmed as part of this story. The highly sensitive might want to read no further.** With apologies, here it is.*

🦋

**Andy and I were** coming home from the *TAG* dance which was held on Saturday nights in the auditorium of Leominster City Hall. It was a well-loved institution for kids of my generation with its dim lighting and a sparkling mirror ball left over from years gone by. A DJ spun little 45 rpm discs with big holes and you spent most of the night building up the nerve to ask the one girl who—through zillions of years of evolution and natural selection—your impeccable instincts had identified as the *one female* in the room *least* likely to dance with you.

Years later I would play with bands at *TAG* but back then it was strictly vinyl on a turntable. Having had enough of our routine humbling for this particular Saturday night, Andy and I headed back to French Hill walking down Mechanic Street under starlight and streetlight the mile-or-so home that seemed a lot further.

It was late when we walked down Vezina Avenue but after crossing Eighth we heard a guttural yowling from the darkness in front of Freddy's house and we slowed our step as we approached. It was a cat that had been hit by a car and it was obvious that its backbone was broken in half because as it struggled to get out of the road, its rear quarters flopped to a different side than the front. Andy and I were both horrified. "We can't leave it like this," he said. I didn't reply but tried to think of a course of action.

Andy went over to someone's trash barrels and came back with a six-foot length of two-by-four. He lifted the board up and tried to hit the poor cat to put it out of its misery but the first strike only glanced it and it wailed in new agony. He tried again and it only made matters worse. I'd had enough of this painful drama so on impulse I jumped up into the air over the cat's head.

&#8471;

*Interlude:*

*Let's leave young, cat-loving John Tata hanging in space for a moment in defiance of gravity. John is perhaps five-foot eight-inches tall and somewhat husky at 150. TAG was not an event to get all gussied up for and both he and Andy were wearing T-shirts and dungarees. On his feet John wears the engineer boots that he had gotten one Christmas as a present—the kind Brando and Dean wore. He had loved the boots so much that he slept with them in his bed that night and had fallen asleep gazing at them as they rested on his pillow. They were big clunky, things with a strap and a buckle, meant for hard work or riding motorcycles; but now they were locked together hovering over this poor cat's head on a balmy starlit night in the Plastic City as the maple leaves gossiped in the darkness above the glow of the streetlights.*

&#8471;

Inevitably gravity prevailed. The end of the cat's suffering was swift. Once the yowling had ended, Vezina Avenue in the late evening became profoundly silent. Andy, still holding the two-by-four, was panting and in shock. I was looking down at the body of the poor creature shocked as well. Suddenly Andy yelled, "Eeeyaahhhh," and he held his left arm out at an odd angle. One of the cat's yellow eyes had popped out of its skull and had stuck to Andy's forearm. *"It's starin' at me,"* he screamed. The eye did seem trained on his face as if in condemnation.

*Jeddah, Kingdom of Saudi Arabia, 1988*

# PINNACLES

**As a kid growing up** in the Plastic City, one of the things I dreamed of doing was what they used to refer to as "Skin Diving" back in the days of the television show *Sea Hunt* starring Lloyd Bridges. I had neither the resources nor the wherewithal to equip and train myself to make the dream a reality so a dream it remained until I eventually stopped dreaming it. During my year of living semi-dangerously in the Kingdom of Saudi Arabia, the fulfillment of that dream was rekindled because I found myself to be living in a divers' paradise: Jeddah—on the Red Sea. The water there is crystal-clear and teaming with marine life. Divers come from around the globe to experience it the way climbers are drawn the Mount Everest. It was a great opportunity for us, the expatriate employees, to pick up the hobby on our time off.

I had been snorkeling with some of the guys from the English school where we were working to develop a custom

English curriculum for Saudi Air Force cadets. When I talked about the Red Sea with Richard (a teacher who also played lead guitar in our band, Exit Only), he was quick to solemnly point out that there were things out there that could actually kill me if I didn't take it seriously. He was an old hand in-country and knew the ropes so whatever wisdom he might impart, I would certainly consider.

You had to be on your guard out there. Among other dangers were the striped sea snakes whose bite was lethal. I learned that their mouths are very small however and that they would have a hard time biting you unless they got you in the fleshy skin between your fingers or toes. In that event you should enjoy your last three or four strokes because they would probably be your last. As this was being explained to me I was wading out to the deeper water at a popular dive site with one of the guys from the school. "Like that one right there," he'd said, pointing down at a black and white viper floating by my leg—dead thankfully.

That very same weekend we were snorkeling off of an abandoned granite pier when I turned around to find a school of Barracudas swimming between me and the dock. They were silvery and sunlit near the surface—and they blocked my path back. These are large and show a LOT of teeth in a kind of five-pound grin. One bit of folklore that had been related to me was that of a Brit who recently had his hand bitten off by a Barracuda when he went to rinse fish guts off his glove from the side of a boat. I treaded water for quite a while until they finally moved on, still smiling their menacing smiles like the baddest gang in the neighborhood.

&

One weekend, which in the Kingdom is a Thursday and Friday, I went out to another well-known dive site called The Pinnacles. I was with Ken; the drummer in Exit Only, and his wife; Wendy, who sang in the group. They had been in the KSA for some time, and were experienced scuba divers happy to mentor me as to how it was done.

We rocked and rolled over the dunes on the way to the site and they were laughing at me because I was convinced that their vintage yellow and white Chevy Blazer was going to roll over and I kept asking Ken to slow down.

There were perhaps 20 vehicles parked on the beach near The Pinnacles when we arrived and divers were coming out, going in or staging to do one or the other. It was a mixed-assortment of Britons and Americans and the way the vehicles were deployed told a story of its own. The Brits had arranged their rigs together with military precision and had lashed tarpaulin tents over the whole affair creating an ad hoc camp site. By comparison, the rest of the SUVs looked tossed-about like a fickle child's toys.

These Limeys introduced me to what would become my beverage of choice while in the Kingdom: the local moonshine nicknamed *Saddeqi* (Arabic for friend) mixed with orange juice. Everybody just swigged it from plastic water bottles. *Saddeqi* straight tastes like nail polish remover smells and is like a double-strength Vodka, but mixed with orange juice it became a proper Screwdriver (as improper as alcohol is in that dry country—*haraam*).

Being there was like being on a very nice beach anywhere on Earth except that when you turned away from the water, instead of seeing honky-tonks, amusement rides, condos, hotels, hotties and traffic—there was nothing but a seemingly infinite expanse of sand. Ken and Wendy hooked me up with some flippers and a mask while they donned their air tanks and we walked out thigh-deep into the Red Sea for about 60 yards to where the underwater terrain dropped precipitously at an 80-foot sheer cliff. I put my mask on and dunked my head under and I could easily see The Pinnacles through the crystalline water.

They were two towers of limestone of at least 70 feet in height and encrusted in coral and other sealife. The divers swimming around them looked tiny from this distance, like guppies in an aquarium. I just sort of snorkeled around while Ken and Wendy swam out to the outcroppings—but there was nothing for me to see—the real attraction was beyond my range.

Wendy came out and asked me if I wanted to go down. She offered me the extra oxygen line from the tank—an "Octopus" she called it—and instructed me to hang on to her buoyancy compensation vest and we breast stroked out to the site. Once there she pushed the *down* button and we sank like an elevator—little Wendy was dragging me under. The water pressure started squeezing my head almost immediately and my natural buoyancy had me upside down and spinning like a fishing lure as we went deeper. There were two finger slots in the mask made for clearing your ears and I stuck my forefinger and thumb into them and blew my nose but it would not clear. Wendy looked up to give me a questioning thumbs-up gesture which I stoically returned. But I was decidedly NOT thumbs-up. My head felt like it was in a vice. When we got back to the cliff, I told her what had happened, downplaying it so as not to hurt her feelings, but I was bleeding from my nostrils and my head was killing me. Wendy had helped me fulfill an old dream—but more's the pity—it died that day. Before long, Ken joined us and as we chatted about the dive, a hubbub arose around us. People were leaving the water rather in panic: it appeared that a shark had approached The Pinnacles. Somebody said that it was a white-tipped specimen some ten feet in length. I stooped—holding the mask to my face and dunked my head under the water. All of the "guppies" had evacuated but the *squalus* was doing excited figure eights around the towers no doubt sniffing for the good eating that had just been swimming there. I stood up to comment but found myself profoundly alone—standing knee-deep in the Red Sea—60 yards from safety—my mask half-filled with blood. Just me and a large, hungry, *Carcharhinus longimanus*—a creature once described as the "most dangerous of all sharks" by Jacques Cousteau.

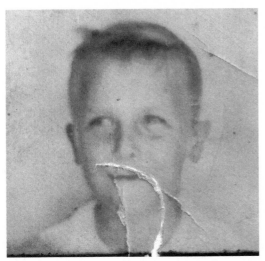
*Photobooth photo from Whalom Park, 1950s*

# THE BOX

*Prelude:*
*I say again: the only things to fear on French Hill in the Fifties were big kids, bigger kids and global thermonuclear war. This small incident illustrates this point pretty clearly, on yet another summer day of which there seemed to be so many with so many left to come when summers seemed to last forever.*

&

**Walking down the hill** on Ninth Street towards home I noticed a commotion at the top of Spruce Street which intersects it. I was curious and still young enough not to be cautious about what I might be walking into, so I climbed up to Tenth and Spruce sipping from the sweating Coke bottle that I'd just bought at Cote's garage.

As I approached, I saw that it was a group big kids perhaps the age of my friend Frankie's big brother Danny. In fact I recognized that it was Danny as I got closer, but no one else did I know. They were surrounding a large industrial-strength wooden box with four heavy casters screwed to the bottom in a diamond pattern. The box had cryptic-looking numbers and words stenciled on the sides in black paint. It might have been five or six-feet-high, five-feet-long and four-feet-wide and the guys were spinning it around. Where it came from remains a complete mystery.

A voice was emanating from inside of it, a little kid's voice screaming to be let out. I thought the talking box was pretty amusing until somebody said, "There's another one," and before I could say *boo* I was unceremoniously tossed over the top and dumped in. I got to my feet and the voice in the box was staring at me, his eyes wide with apprehension. He was my age but I didn't know him. When a third kid tumbled in we all stared at each other uncomprehendingly like rats in a trap. It was too high to reach the top so all we could do was gaze longingly at the rectangle of free blue sky above us.

When we felt the box being rolled into position and pushed down the hill, we all started pounding on the walls trying to avoid the nails and yelling at the tops of our lungs. You could feel that deathtrap pick up momentum as it barreled down Tenth but we were blinded and hadn't a clue as to where we were going. The box was going at a pretty high rate of speed until near the bottom it violently wobbled a few times and then flipped over. We were tossed onto the hot tar and tumbled out like three dice from a craps cup.

We got to our feet and looked back up the hill. The guys were laughing and actually had the gall to wave us back for another ride. Even from that distance I could see that Danny was drinking from my Coke bottle. We answered them with our middle fingers and the saltiest epithets that we could muster at that young age so naturally they made as if to chase after us. We ran for our lives in our individual directions home.

Despite our shared ordeal—in the rest of my many years on French Hill—I never saw my fellow dice after that day.

*The crucifix at Saint Cecilia's*

# CENTENARIAN

**In December of 2011**, when I made my annual pilgrimage to Leominster and Fitchburg to visit my mother's final resting place, for the first time I was accompanied by my wife Jocelyn. We'd begun by visiting my old house of course and then Saint Cecilia's church. The same *crèche* that had graced the altar rail in my youth had been set up yet again. The figurines all looked familiar much to my amazement. I dropped a coin into a statuette of a kneeling brother and he nodded mechanically in recognition of my donation. Then my attention turned to the nave overall.

In my youth, the windows had been stained a somber amber hue, but now they had been redone with colorful religious imagery which to me, although beautiful, seem to lack the *gravitas* of the old color scheme. Another new item is a lovely life-size statue of a newly-martyred, and rather fetching-in-her-repose, Saint Cecilia, laying on what looks to be a sarcophagus.

This patron saint of musicians points toward Heaven in a final act of defiance as she dies for her faith. The *bas-relief* stations-of-he-cross looked just as I remembered them rendered in lifelike 3-D.

Although the church is usually empty when I come, I always sense other human presences nearby, just out of sight backstage somewhere, clearing their throats or conversing in low tones. And there is always *one* lone figure, hunched in prayer, somewhere in the nave.

As I move about, my footsteps echo in the cavernous building. A parishioner of Saint Cecelia's had carved a life-size and extremely realistic statue of Jesus on the cross back when I was a young churchgoer and he had donated it to the parish. I pointed out to my wife that it was at first over to the right of the altar mounted on a column but over the years I have seen it moved to the center behind the altar mounted on cheap-looking siding. Eventually they got it right and it now hangs suspended over the altar: the church's centerpiece.

I had seen on local television news that the sculptor, Louis Chapentier, was still active and carving at 100 and I had gotten it into my head that I might like to buy a smaller version of that crucifix that I had always admired. With a little help from a letter carrier pounding his beat we found our way to Louis' house up on Merriam Avenue. It wasn't hard to notice because it being just after Christmas, the front yard of his modest ranch was festooned with whimsical Christmas-themed Styrofoam carvings, all of his own design. While Jocelyn scrutinized the figures, I went up and pressed not one but two doorbells per the note on the door. He came out and I introduced myself and stated why I had come. He warmly invited me in as if he had been expecting drop-in company (which I suspect he is used to). I called back for Jocelyn to join me as I went in.

The house was warm and inviting and sunlight shafted in through the windows. We'd interrupted him: seems he'd been doing a little ironing. He was dressed very neatly and wore his signature bow tie and a sweater vest. He is slight in stature (five-feet-tall?) and 125 pounds wringing-wet, if that. He's not at all wrinkled, has all his hair and his seeing and hearing were just fine as far as I could tell. He smiled welcomingly as my wife came in and asked him how old he was. He stood up straight like a well-prepared student and reported proudly, "I'm 100 years old" with a slight French-Canadian accent. Jocelyn had to go over and hug him and kiss him on one of his apple cheeks (something which I suspect he is also used to). He started giving us a rundown of his life and I sensed him gauging the amount of time we had and streamlining his story to accommodate our time frame (that being I wanted to get to my mother's resting place so that I could place a pot of Poinsettias before the sun went down).

He took us around the house and showed us his work. They were mostly dioramas carved from wood, Styrofoam and clear Lucite depicting historical scenes, vignettes from his own life way up in northern French-speaking Canada and nature vignettes showing animals hunting one another in the wild. He had a way of going into a little trance and saying, "He's only trying to get something to eat..." pointing at a fox taking down a rabbit, almost quizzically, as if forgiving the predator's fundamental nature. He repeated the statement while standing before several of his sculptures.

"If you like I can take you down to my shop and show you how I work," he said, but I was a little hesitant to accept the offer, because of schedule...and maybe something else. He showed us pencil drawings of celebrities and a Happy Birthday letter from President Obama. Louis' work looked like it should be at the *Smithsonian* as a national treasure.

After we had looked at everything in the house he once again offered to take us into the cellar to show us his process and this time Jocelyn accepted. With some reservations I followed them down the stairs. The cellar was divided into two chambers and the workshop had a solid door. He switched on the light on the outside as we went in. Louis pointed out some works in progress and then sat down at his bench to show us his carving lathe which is his treasure. It was close and dim in that old cellar and I was bumping my head on objects hanging from the rafters. Tools and wooden objects in assorted stages of completion lay everywhere and the only light came from one small overhead fixture. He showed us a piece he had just begun working on: another, though smaller crucifix than the one at the church. The wood that he was using seemed to be a scrap from an old house, perhaps a piece of a porch, but when he cradled it in his hands, the emerging form became evident—the head, torso and bent legs: the unmistakable image of Our Lord and Savior on the cross. Then he did something inexplicable...

*"Now if you'll excuse me for just a second, I have something else I want to show you," and he hopped from his stool with remarkable dexterity and went out the door. He turned as he did and said, "I hope you enjoy my cellar," with his pleasantly apple-cheeked smiling face, and then slamming the door and turning out the light. As his feet stomped up the stairs, Jocelyn and I stood in stunned silence. We stared at each other blindly but the darkness was too profound for us to see. I felt my way over and tried the door but it was locked and felt solid. I went into damage-control mode. "Okay," I thought, "the room is full of tools so I ought to be able to get out of here if I...."*

...but none of that really happened. What happened in reality was that he demonstrated his lathing technique on a little piece of scrap wood, a floral pattern that he signed, dated and graciously handed to my Jocelyn. I got the feeling that he could have gone on all night long. As we put our coats on, I spoke with him about the price of a smaller version of the crucifix at Saint Cecilia's. He did not have any in stock so it would be a custom-order and I told him I would get back to him.

&

*Coda:*

*Where I attended elementary grades one through six (Spruce Street School) now stands a high-rise senior citizen apartment tower ("come hooommmmeeee Johneeeeee, back to schoooollll...").*

*Across the street had stood, and still stands, Bob Desilet's market. We didn't have a car when I was growing up and Bob would send a kid over on a bicycle to deliver the groceries that my mother had phoned in. I'd thought of making a sentimental stop there during past pilgrimages because Desilet's Market was still printed on the awning, but I always chickened out. Jocelyn gave me the guts to go in this time and the plan was to buy a meat pie and a Poutine which are French-Canadian delicacies. Bob's youngest son was now running the store and I chatted with him as he prepared our order.*

*I was kind of disappointed that he did not remember the time that I went with him and his brothers to see the* Cisco Kid's Wild West Show *at the Boston Garden a million years ago. "If you say so," he had said, turning around to his regular customers to share the joke. He did remember Mrs. Tata though which made me feel better.*

*Jocelyn and I ate the meat pie the following morning which was a Sunday. It tasted okay but I felt kind of funny after I'd eaten it and wished that I hadn't. I think that what bothered me was that the contents were just listed as being "meat." For us at least, the Poutine also proved to be an acquired taste that we failed to acquire.*

*As far as the special-order crucifix is concerned, I did not get back to him, much to my regret. He passed away on June 3, 2015 at the age of 104. He is a legend in the Plastic City and was greatly honored by its citizens during his later years. I'm happy that I got a chance to meet him. God speed Louis.*

*1971*

# DOCTOR WU

*Prelude:*
*My muse has been nagging me to write an amusing (hopefully) story about working a part-time job at a furniture store one morning, long ago, stuffing beans into beanbag chairs. I have it sketched out in my memory—after all, I've told it a lot over the years—but I can't start it yet because of the thing that once grew in my throat. The reason that I was working two jobs at that time was because I was trying to recover, financially and physically, from an illness—and I can't seem to find a way to write about that in an abbreviated form. So here instead is a more somber story. It wants to be told and I'm sorry but there seems to be no way around it.*

&

**The thing started out**, I suppose, as something microscopic in size imbedded in my throat. It proceeded to grow to the size of a grain of salt, perhaps a BB, up to a pea, and then a grape. It was on its way to being the size of a walnut with a license-to-kill by the time I was admitted to the hospital, and growing by leaps and bounds. Prior to that, the ever-worsening symptoms of its existence were my labored breathing and congestion. It got to the point where I had to sleep sitting up to avoid drowning from it. My face swelled up on the right side pulling my eye socket over giving me the look of a Sumo wrestler. But not a fat Sumo for my weight had fallen to under 150 over the course of the winter; pretty skinny for me. In addition, my skin had begun to develop a grayish cast. Not being able to diagnose that I had this growing mass in my throat, our old-school family doctor put me on a strict regimen of Karo Syrup and Canada Mints.

In desperation I followed someone's advice and saw a sinus specialist. His name was Dr. Wu—like in the Steely Dan song. He swabbed my sinus cavities and they checked out, but he said he didn't like the sound of my cough and ordered up an X-ray which I had the following day.

The day following that Dr. Wu called me at the food warehouse where I worked to give me the results of the X-ray. The number I had left him was for the old black payphone on the wall of the employee entrance. My boss, Guido, answered and had called me over. The voice on the other side of the line told me that I had a tumor. I was speechless for a moment while I absorbed the news until he broke the silence and asked, "Do you understand me Mr. Tata?" in his thick Chinese accent. I'd have to get myself into a hospital and fast too because I was now racing against the tumor's growth. I hung the handset back onto its hook switch and went back to picking my store orders of Surefine green beans, Niblets and Dinty Moore Beef Stew.

⚬

A doctor named Clark was assigned to my case once I'd been admitted to the Worcester Memorial Hospital. He poked and prodded at what had now become a very pronounced bump just under my Adam's apple with a look of concern. He pulled my then wife Susan aside in the corridor to warn her to brace herself because if this thing was what it looked to be; I might not be around much longer. He even went so far as to suggest that it might be better if I didn't know at all. But she knew me well enough to know that it couldn't be kept from me and told him so. Upon hearing the bleak prognosis, I assured her that despite appearances, I felt that I was going to be okay, just based on faith I guess. It seemed ironic though that if my instinct proved false, I might be following my teenage idol, James Dean, down the dark highway and at the same tender age of 24.

I waited for my appointment with the scalpel, warmed by the shafts of sunlight angling through the big windows of the old wing of the hospital. A guy in the bed next to mine was having a bypass and I suppose because I looked trustworthy, he handed his expensive-looking watch to me for safekeeping prior to his operation. I slid it onto my wrist and assured him that I would look after it. When he came out of surgery he was kind of groggy but we still managed to chat a bit. He opened his pajama shirt to show me his chest. He had a row of thick stitches from neck-to-navel. The scar looked new and raw and he gaped at it in bewilderment. It reminded me of the stitching of a football. I gave him back his watch and he put it on—a first step towards recovery.

In those days I drove a 1966 Thunderbird that was nice but temperamental about starting. Susan was a fledgling driver and Worcester from the Plastic City was a stretch when she came to visit. On at least one occasion, I needed to get up and sneak out of the hospital to try to start it so that she could get home. There was a trick to it. The day before surgery a priest came in and took my confession and later that evening Susan visited. She had smuggled in a bottle of wine and we toasted to life out of little throw-away paper cups from the water cooler.

After two days in the hospital they wheeled me into the operating room. The plan was to cut into my Lymph gland, biopsy a bit of tissue, and if it was cancerous, go in and cut the tumor out of my throat. An entire operating team was suited-up and ready to swing into action upon the word from the lab. Probably woozy from Valium I cracked jokes with them about missing my breakfast Frosted Flakes as we all waited for the results of the test. After a while they broke down and wheeled me back to my room. There would be no operation. Dr. Clark told me that the results had showed that this type of tumor was treatable with radiation: a Medial-Sternal Mass he had called it. "If you have to have a tumor, this is a good kind to have," he'd assured me.

I immediately went into radiation (Cobalt) therapy. They drew target markers on my neck and blasted away at the tumor which started shrinking almost immediately. Dr. Clark had me stay in the hospital for a while in the event that the tumor might do something unpredictable but fortunately for me it didn't swell—it went down and stayed down. They kept me in intensive care while they observed how the tumor would respond to the radiation but my faith had been rewarded, I was going to be okay. I was however run down and weakened. The doctor told me that I should get myself onto Social Security disability. He wouldn't advise me to return to work...*ever*. I had been officially pronounced out-of-commission.

*My Thunderbird*

# THE PATCH

**The tumor in my throat** had been brought under control by the Cobalt treatments and I was on disability—and on orders from my doctor—permanently. But those checks didn't add up to enough to pay our expenses and since I was feeling a lot better, I went back to my job at Associated Grocers. I was a Teamster again and I had maintained my seniority so when I returned I got onto a forklift which was a much nicer job than hand-picking orders, but did so wearing a mask out of concern that the dust would aggravate my lungs. I'd had to cancel my disability claim of course, and although the warehouse job paid decent working man's wages, I had fallen behind financially.

I was on the two-to-ten shift which gave me open time in the morning, and I was able to find a job at a somewhat low-rent furniture store in "The Patch" section of Fitchburg, not far from the perennially closed Fifth Street bridge. The store was called Giovani's and it was Mr. Giovani himself that hired me to help around the store eight-until-noon. He was a decent guy to work for. Mr. G. favored Italian sport jackets, drove an enormous moss-green El Dorado convertible and always had a tan. His Tudor-style brick house was up on the tonier side of the Plastic City on Route 13 neighboring my Uncle Dom's ranch. He could get to screaming at you in his operatic tenor if he thought you were screwing off or giving him any shit whatsoever. I'd seen it demonstrated and made sure not to piss him off—easier to do when you're only there for four hours a day. I was the easy employee—quick-in-and-out. I suppose that it's standard operating procedure, but whenever he sold a lamp, he always remembered to unscrew the lightbulb and stick it into his jacket pocket with an impish grin. This always made me shake my head in disbelief. I mean, couldn't you just *give* these poor slobs the bulb for God's sake?

It became a little game for Mr. G. to find something for me to do every workday. Mostly I helped shuffle furniture around the showroom creating little vignettes where the pieces would look attractive together (and people could visualize them in their own homes), loading the delivery truck or screwing kitchen table tops to their legs with a hand screwdriver. One time at a loss, he handed me an ice chopper and I spent my four hours out in the parking lot hacking away at a big late-winter chunk of frozen snow shaped like that one that sank the Titanic.

One particular morning when I punched in, he was standing by the clock, sizzling his palms together, obviously waiting for me. He had a perfect project. I followed him down into the gloomy cellar of the old Victorian commercial building. The structure had a brick foundation and a dirt floor with a fine coat of talcum powder-like dust the color of cocoa. I remember thinking that my footprints in the dust reminded me of the ones the astronauts had left on the moon. Cobwebs hung from the rafters high above me as thick as cheesecloth—rippling subtly with the slightest breeze. This tomb was lit by a dangling fluorescent light with three of its four rods out, buzzing and crackling away. He pointed at a wall of neatly stacked square cartons.

"This order of beanbag chairs was delivered last month and has been sitting here ever since," he explained. "I can't sell them because they came in too understuffed. I needed to order some more beans from the manufacturer to beef 'em up and they came in Tuesday," he went on to say. He cracked open a carton and pulled out a sad-looking electric-blue blob of vinyl with a zipper on its side and plopped it at my feet. He pointed at a cardboard 55-gallon drum and an aluminum pail sitting next to it and said, "Those are the beans. Take the beans out of the barrel using the pail and fatten up the chairs—easy?"

After I nodded he climbed the flight of wooden stairs to the main showroom floor. He turned around at the top, silhouetted by the light and said, "That should keep you busy for a while." Although his face was in shadow, I knew that he had that little lightbulb-snatching impish grin on his face. With that he shut the door.

Save for the sputtering of the fluorescent lamp it fell silent. Now it was just me, the wall of cases and whatever my fertile imagination might conjure up from the shadows of this morbid cellar...

*...as from behind long-forgotten bins and barrels, decaying corpses laboriously dragged themselves from the dust of their shallow graves and began to shamble towards my back—seeking life—**hungering** for life—putrefying flesh dangling from their cadaverous limbs like fetid rags as they blindly clawed through the cobweb curtains to...*

Purposefully not looking over my shoulder, I stooped over and unzipped the chair which revealed that the beans inside were actually balls of Styrofoam about the size of peas. I pried open the drum and it was in fact full of the same kind of "beans." I then picked up the pail and gouged it into the barrel and pulled out a load. The Styrofoam balls were so charged with static electricity that they not only filled the pail but coated the outside as well as my hands and arms. I pulled open the slot in the chair and started to pour the balls in but they resisted. They would not come out of the pail. I needed to start clawing them out and stuffing them into the bags. The vinyl had its own static charge going on and it seemed that the only place the beans wanted to be was anywhere but in the bags.

I used to like to wear bib overalls to work in those days and my hair was long (more static). I couldn't see myself but I must have looked like the Pillsbury Doughboy. I was spitting them out and trying not to inhale them. Unfortunately the morning was going by and I hadn't been able to finish the first chair. There were almost as many beans dancing on the outside of it as there were on the inside—not very attractive as a sales item I'm afraid. There was no question in my mind that Mr. G. was going to find this unacceptable, so I did what I could, sealed a few cartons back up and announced that I was leaving for the day—a day which I knew would be my last day, and I was happy that I'd be missing the boss's withering tenor.

⚿

*Coda:*

*Those overalls with all of their compartments were probably never again completely free of Styrofoam balls. Beans were in my socks and my shoes. I was pulling them out of my hair, my ears and from between my toes. A month later I even found one in my navel.*

*Magnolia, 2001*

# NINE ONE ONE

*Prelude:*
*Osama was dead: to begin with. There's no doubt about that.*
*Regardless of what other jacks might pop out of the big sandbox—*
*color this bogeyman gone. I got this news on my commute to work*
*and was surprised to have cold and bitter tears coat my eyes. They*
*were certainly not for that bloody-handed bastard, that much I*
*knew. My guess is that the news brought back forgotten or repressed*
*memories from the time of the September 11th attacks and the*
*emotions that accompanied them.*

*In the Eighties I saw a Beatles tribute show in Boston called*
Beatlemania. *Then too, I had been emotionally touched by the*
*those sights and sounds from the beginning of the previous decade*
*and their attendant baggage.*

**Two Brides**
**I did not, as a rule**, travel for my company. With the

exception of my year in Saudi Arabia and handful of overseas assignments, I worked in the same office, commuting on Route 128 day-after-day and had for many years. However in September of 2001, the company needed someone to fill in for a designer who worked in its Roslyn, Virginia office—just across the Potomac from DC, up on Wilson Boulevard. She was taking two weeks off to get married and have a honeymoon. On a lark, and wishing to visit the capital, I volunteered.

I made it clear that on the middle weekend, my stepdaughter was getting married back home in Magnolia and that as father-of-the-bride, my presence would be required. They approved that and I flew down to Roslyn to meet up with this other bride-to-be. While she ran through my responsibilities and what I might encounter while I filled in for her, I observed that although she was technically a graphic designer the same as me, this operation was more of a revision and quick copy center for presentations and not my forte whatsoever. But while I worked with her for the day before returning home for my own little wedding, it seemed like everything was under control. I should have worried more.

⚓

On that middle weekend, I flew back to walk my Alyson down the aisle. While riding over to the little chapel of Saint Joseph's (since demolished) in the limousine, time seemed to slow to a hallucinatory crawl. She asked the question that I had been thinking, "Doesn't this seem to be taking an awfully long time?" I can't account for it but it sure seemed to take more than the five minutes it should have taken to drive to St. Joe's. It was what I like to call an "Einstein Thing." After what seemed like an eternity, we marched (rather hurriedly) down the short aisle to the familiar strains of Wagner. Later, at the reception, I managed to give a little speech through the DJ's sound system and then, since the ham in me can't resist an audience, I plugged in my Gibson and warbled a couple of Elvis songs for good measure

## Nine One One

With my stepfatherly duties now fulfilled, my personal honeymoon from work had ended as well and on Monday I departed once again for DC from Logan airport. I was really impressed by how blithe this shuttle flight was—this on the day before air travel would become anything but. During the ascent, my ears popped and then plugged. To add to my discomfort, my metal-framed glasses lost a screw and I had jerry-rigged the stem to the frame with my niece's earring.

After landing, I went down to the baggage carousel to collect the huge suitcase containing another week's worth of clean shirts. After I'd been waiting there for a while, a skycap rolled in a cart loaded with a dozen or so black bags, unloaded them and walked off. After waiting for quite a while for the carousel to start up, I gave up hope and walked over to a little office to find someone to ask questions of. I then noticed that my suitcase was there on the floor. There weren't enough bags to bother with the carousel so they just wheeled them in on a cart. Shuttle flyers travel light.

I picked up my rental, a red Chevy Blazer and drove over to the Francis Scott Key Marriot to register. The room had a panoramic view of the Potomac languidly rolling by in the overcast with the towers of Georgetown University silhouetted in the darkening sky—red warning lights flashing atop their spires. I ordered room service and got a good night's sleep.

Monday began horrendously. I didn't know how to find the files, and the color Xerox in the office was temperamental to say the least. I could sense the customers becoming skeptical. I was out of my water and sinking fast but was determined to get done what needed to get done, whatever it took. But all-in-all it was one of the worst workdays of my life and I felt terribly incompetent. When I got back to the room that night I literally got down on my knees and asked God to help me.

**Pentagon**

Tuesday started strong however. I was in early and parked in the building's garage. I'd located the *good* coffee (the kind that gets its own little corrugated jacket) and armed with that, made my way through the labyrinthine series of doors, passwords and *Secret Squirrel* shit that gains you access into the office. I sat down at my desk and booted up the PC. It was 8 a.m., September 11, 2001 and I was finally starting to settle down a bit.

&

At 9:43 a.m. I heard a muffled thump that to me sounded like the elevator car banging around in its shaft. This was followed by some high-pitched feminine squealing that I took to be lighthearted fun. Then it went back to the quiet again. My office was in the bowels of the sixth floor away from any windows. I had my door cracked about two inches hoping to dissuade anyone from bringing me any more work while not shutting them out entirely. By this point the customer flow had slowed to a trickle anyway. They were obviously hunkering down and making due until the return of their *Trusted One*.

I heard some running footsteps in the hall and looked up to see the two IT guys (who had helped me with my printer) go flying by the crack in the door but thought little of it. A second later one of them came back, a young kid with dyed-yellow hair and a cheap looking tie. He didn't open the door but spoke through the crack, looking like he was wrestling with an impulse to become totally unglued. "They've bombed the Pentagon and the World Trade towers, *we're evacuating the building*" he said sounding a lot like Gene Wilder. "C'mon, we have to **go!**" I have to give him credit for doubling back like that. If he hadn't, I probably would have sat there working all day in an empty building. As I followed them down the hall, I could see the Pentagon burning through the windows. We passed the common kitchen area where a television was showing the World Trade Center with black smoke billowing up at a 45-degree angle.

Now there was my Blazer to retrieve from the parking garage. In hindsight I should have left it there and walked down the hill to the hotel but instead I waited as the lot attendants tried to rush everybody out all at the same time. It seemed like an eternity but they did a great job. Out on Wilson Boulevard you had to make a right because of the traffic. The streets were clogged with cars. The only thing to do was to go with the flow which would be a right and another right and try to get to Fort Myers Drive and to my hotel. I turned onto the Jefferson Davis Highway which the military had already blocked because of its proximity to the Pentagon. This meant a right on Marshall Drive and another onto North Meade Street in the vicinity of Arlington Cemetery. These turns looped me around the park that holds the Marine Corps statue, the one where they are planting the flag on Mount *Suribachi* on Iwo-Jima. When I passed it I looked back over my shoulder and it was quite a sight to see that famous image (and for the first time I might add) with the smoke from the Pentagon rising directly behind it. I was finally working some sightseeing into my visit but it was not what I was expecting.

&

It was a magically beautiful day which is something that everyone seems to remember about 9/11. It only served to make the events more surreal. In a heightened state of awareness, I noticed a few things that stand out as vignettes in my memory. There was young woman pushing a baby carriage around the park in a very determined, almost manic way. I kept seeing her because she would keep catching up to me the stop-and-go traffic. I saw a young heavy-set, long-haired white kid shucking and jiving down the sidewalk looking just overjoyed at the chaos. A civilian car, obviously driven by law-enforcement, was forcing its way through the intersection at Fairfax and Meade—its driver standing on the horn. There were evacuated office workers in summery clothing looking up apprehensively at the unfamiliar sound of F-15s passing low overhead and I remember thinking at that moment that this must be the sound of a war starting. I noticed one couple clearly. They looked like office lovers, whose movie-like romance was being sullied by this messy surprise.

I made my way back to the hotel, switched on the television and sat at the desk to jot down some notes. Those nightmarish visions of the fires and smoke—people running for their lives—buildings falling into dust, were almost too much to bear in the gloom of my drape-darkened room. I was sitting at a desk that also supported the large television only inches from my face. It was like witnessing the evisceration of a still-living beast. I guess I succumbed to the impulse to be with others during a time like this and navigated my way down to the bar. It was packed with shell-shocked looking people with drinks in their hands, milling around staring glassy-eyed at the most conveniently located screens. Once that got old I went back to my room and I called my home office. They told me that I could cut short the assignment if I chose and head home since the Roslyn office would probably be closed for a while until everybody figured out how this was all going to shake out. I decided to wait and call in the following morning to find out what the situation actually was going to be.

❧

**Georgetown**

With this unexpected time off, it was finally my time to "experience the nation's capital" as a tourist at last. I headed off on my first order of business which was seeing the spot where the exteriors for my favorite movie, *The Exorcist,* were filmed. The location, I knew, was directly across the Francis Scott Key Bridge in Georgetown so I just walked over, foregoing the rental vehicle. Black smoke was still rising from the Pentagon but nobody walking on the bridge seemed to look in its direction except for me. Everybody seemed oblivious to it to tell the truth. I wandered around a bit in the neighborhood where

I thought the address was, walking up and down the street looking at the facades. There was a couple selling guidebooks from a makeshift stand that was ignoring me until I asked if they knew which house had been used in the movie. Strange as it seems, they didn't. A jogger came by and they asked her if she knew. Jogging in place she pointed at the one she thought it was but wouldn't bet the farm on it. I stood and gawked at the house for a minute then climbed down and then back up the infamous stairs where Father Karras sacrifices himself with a suicidal dive onto them to save Regan's soul from the demon Pazuzu at the film's climax. With my sightseeing tour of DC now complete, I made my way back to the hotel, ordered room service, got loaded and crashed.

&

I called the Roslyn office on the following morning fully expecting it to be closed but was surprised to be told in *no uncertain terms* that it was "business as usual." I drove the big Blazer up to the office but parked in an outside lot rather than in the building for fear of getting trapped again. I was wrapping up everything that I had been working on when I got a call from the woman whom I had been filling in for. She was checking in on how things were going. I filled her in, difficulties and all, and she volunteered that she'd be happy to come back to work a little early to let me off the hook. I told her it wasn't really necessary but she'd had enough of honeymooning I guess and was anxious to get back to her routine (and pee on the bushes I suppose).

So the next day I checked out of the Marriott. No planes or trains were running and I was going to have to drive the bulky SUV back to Massachusetts. I asked for directions in the hotel office and they kindly printed out a *Mapquest* map with about eight pages of text directions and a one-inch square map with a squiggly line between DC and Boston. I looked it over but decided it wasn't going to do me any good with its detailed instructions like...*after curb, drive 12 yards east on Elm, then....*

I'd never get out of the capital that way, so I threw the sheaf onto the shotgun seat. When I got to the parking garage exit, I asked the attendant what the best way to get back to Boston was. He pointed up the street and said, "Okay: go up to the second set of lights and take a left."

"Okay," I said.

"Then go down to the second set of lights and take another left," in his from-someplace-in-Africa accent.

"Uh-huh," I said, nodding.

"Go straight," he went on, "until you see signs for 495 then follow them back to Boston."

⅜

*Coda:*

*It was a long and exhausting drive, but those short and sweet directions got me back home. I had—during this escape from DC—seen the smoke rising from the Pentagon in the morning as well as from what had once been the World Trade towers when I looked back over my shoulder at Manhattan that afternoon, negotiating the Tappan-Zee Bridge across a brown and roiling Hudson river—shocked to my bones.*

*Child of the 1950s*

# THE BARN

**One of my best friends** in youth was a kid named Frankie. He was a year or two older than I, skinny with curly blond hair. He was very cool—modest and funny. Even in the earliest days that I knew him he had a pack-a-day *jones* for filterless Lucky Strikes. His family lived at the corner of Spruce and Eleventh streets, the outer boundary of French Hill before it ended abruptly with a precipitous descent into the valley etched by the grey Nashua.

Frankie was raised to hunt by his father. They seemed to live closer to the earth than did my family without question. Although they dwelled in a house typical of that era and place, it would not be unusual for them to have a few deer hides in the sun-dappled backyard stretched across wooden frames, curing in the sun. It seemed comical to me that Frankie one day had a tiny chipmunk pelt, stretched on popsicle sticks, curing next to the deer hides. Like father like son. At my request, he showed me what he did with the skinned carcass. The poor pink thing was in the trash can looking embarrassingly denuded. The family even had a ridiculous-looking Basset Hound named *Belle* whom Frankie occasionally lifted up by her forepaws and took a Tango around the yard while singing the Vaughn Monroe hit: "Dance *Belle*-erina Dance." Belle would have one of those dog smiles that they get.

Maybe there was something in the drinking water or fumes from the grey river, but there sure were a lot of guitar pickers on "The Hill." Frankie played as did his big brother Danny. Danny's axe was a Danelectro and he had written his name under the clear pickguard with what looked like lipstick and even though it was smeared a little, I thought it was cool as hell.

Frankie and another friend, Ronnie, both seemed to have an impulse to live like mountain men or even Native Americans. There was something survivalist and a desire to be close to the earth about them. I can see those two descending the valley wall on a path that began right in Frankie's backyard—rifles shouldered—on a hunt long before the floodplain became clogged with chain stores.

The field on Twelfth that had once served as our portal to that floodplain had become civilized by a proper Little League playing field complete with a diamond and enclosed by a fence. As much as I resented its intrusion, I had to admit that it looked pretty professional. When we weren't playing sandlot ball there ourselves, we sometimes watched the officiated games. I was there with Frankie one summer day and we were talking with a kid who had a pet squirrel. This thing was on his shoulders, his head, in his pockets and in his shirt. He had peanuts in his pockets and he was feeding it. It was really tame and I would have loved to have had one of my own.

☙

Summer turned to fall and baseball season ended. School had already begun when Frankie approached me excitedly. In his travels he had discovered a barn that had a squirrel nest up on the loft. He wanted to go in and grab a bunch of the kits to train as pets.

With visions of the boy at the baseball field, I hiked out to the barn with Frankie. It was silent inside and smelled of hay and manure. Sunlight beamed in through the cracks and holes of the little-used building and dust motes danced in their light. We were nervous in our bellies as we approached the nest because this was someone's property and we had no business trespassing. There was a weathered ladder to the platform and we climbed up. The parent squirrels were absent and six kits writhed on soft leaves blindly waiting for their next meal. They were younger than I had envisioned and their fur was not yet fully grown in, but they were cute and Frankie and I each snatched up three then scurried down the ladder and to the door of the barn.

Suddenly we heard a shrill screech behind us: **the mother had come back**. She tore up the nest looking for her babies but they were gone. Then she saw us and took off after us. It seems funny to think of running away from a squirrel but run we did because the fury of her charge was not to be denied. She chased us to a few yards beyond the barn door and then stopped and glared after us as we left. I looked back at her and her little face was a mask of horror, anger, indignation and hopelessness. The mother squirrel knew where her boundaries were and she would go no further. We cradled our booty back over the floodplain and toward French Hill.

&

What I had hoped was that Frankie would be able to keep them in a cage in his yard—my three and his—but when he went into the house to ask permission from his parents the answer was no. They were trying to get rid of the pesky squirrels they had already, not get new ones. Frankie came out and gave me the disappointing news and I paused and waited for reality to change—but it wouldn't. They were the animal people and it didn't seem fair, but in the end I lugged *all* six kits over to my house.

My mother was not overly-enthused with the prospect of those rat-like things in her house but soft touch that she was, she allowed me to keep them in the cellar. Since it was becoming colder, she suggested that I bed them in a cardboard box on top of the furnace boiler for a little warmth. I lined the cut-off box with a towel and tried to keep the little things comfortable. At her suggestion I fed them with watered-down milk through an eye dropper and they seemed to take it the best they could. In fact their fur seemed to start filling in and they may even have grown a bit, but one day when I went to feed them they had all stopped breathing. I checked again later and one of them had revived so I gave it a little milk but that was the last gasp—they were all gone.

&#x221E;

*Coda:*

*Frankie fell off my radar after that as we orbited different stars. When I was perhaps 16, I got word that he had succumbed to lung cancer. He was only 18 when he died. The way the story went was that when they wheeled him down the corridor of the hospital after his treatments, he'd been so irradiated that the televisions in the rooms would go on the fritz when he rolled past.*

*Me and Dennis*

# FAIRMOUNT

**Although it may not have** been on the preferred list of potential band venues, the Fairmount Café was always a place where you could get a gig when you had nothing else. It was in a rundown neighborhood of Fitchburg called Cleghorn. If you played there on a Saturday night, part of the job was to back up strippers. We were just a little four-piece rock band and the only appropriate music that we could handle were Blues jams. These extrapolations could go pretty long and I was getting good on bass from trying to find inventive runs within the Pentatonic scale to keep things interesting. But the dancers would grow tired of trying to get us to play with more "boom-**boomba**-boom" in our beat and after a while they started coming with their own decks and cassettes of music that was better-suited to their routines. On one such Saturday when the stripper took to the tiny tiles of the dance floor, we left the stage, relieved of duty, and nestled into the well-worn wooden booths along with everybody else to watch her act.

This was at a time when "exotic dancers" typically peeled

down only so far because of *Ye Auld Blue Laws of Massachusetts.* This particular girl could be coaxed into pushing the envelope if prompted enthusiastically enough by her audience, and on this night she would do just that. She danced to four songs becoming less clothed during each one.

The pacing of the show was in fits and starts though because in the interest of protecting her wardrobe, she would run back to the hall near the ladies' room and hang up each article of apparel as she shed them. For her finale, she went from table to table twirling red tassels that she'd somehow adhered to her breasts. It was kind of like a dual-prop P-38 buzzing the table tops and it was a "great effect" to quote Benjamin in *The Graduate.*

When she got to our booth she paused to show the trick off when this nimrod at the table reached out and yanked a tassel off which produced a *pop* loud enough to be audible over the music. She stopped in her tracks and glared at this jerk in stunned disbelief. As the other tassel pendulated the guy reached over and snapped it off too for good measure, then he sat back and crossed his arms in a defiant gesture. Outraged, she grabbed one of the empty longnecks on the table (of which there were about 20) and smashed it over his head. Before he could utter a complaint she laid another one across his skull. As she reached for a third he broke and ran which involved jumping over the table because he was hemmed in by people. She threw the third dead soldier at him and connected with his head yet again. She was winding up for a fourth shot but by then he was gone like a *cooooool breeeeeze.*

&

As we got ready to start our last Rock set, the stripper gathered up her boom box and items of costume then made for the door. We noticed that she'd left a pair of her feathery high heels behind and I enthusiastically volunteered to follow her out and return them. A huge El Dorado of an indistinguishable color was idling across Fairmount Street in a frosty drizzle under a streetlight. I ski-skated up the sidewalk and the front passenger window jiggled down. An enormous African-American gentleman leaned over and regarded me with eyeballs the size of hard-boiled eggs from behind the steering wheel. "Whatchoowan?" he asked in a *basso profondo*. I smiled sheepishly—mutely held up the shoes and he nodded. The front window jiggled up as the back one slid down. I handed her the shoes and she said thanks but I didn't really see anything of her except for one glammed up hand. I walked back into the club through the slush and looked back as the caddy lumbered off.

☙

*Coda:*

*At the end of the evening the band was sitting at a table near the front window unwinding as the crowd put on their coats and filed out into the slush. It always reminded me of sitting in a bathtub and watching the water drain out.*

*Suddenly something rapped loudly against the window and then fell on the sidewalk with a tinkling of glass. A plume of fire six-feet-tall erupted outside. We scrambled out to investigate as the club owner ran out to douse the fire with an extinguisher. Apparently someone had tossed a Molotov cocktail at the building for reasons of their own. Just another day in the neighborhood... and we ain't talkin' no Mr. Rogers.*

*My mirror*

# FLYER COMET

**The party on Lake Whalom** was in full-swing. It was happening at a cottage opposite the amusement park that took the lake's name as its own. This was during the only period in my life that I could actually say that I made a living—meager though it may have been—as a musician. The Katzenjammer Kids played music together and hung out a lot when they didn't. There were a lot of familiar faces at the party that Saturday night and I felt at ease. The party's host approached me as I stood talking with our drummer; Chuck (not his name) and his brother; Ricky (not his name either).

The host extended his right hand palm-up and opened his fingers magician-like revealing four small shapes that looked like little brown beetles laying there belly-up. *Hors d'oeuvres* were being served. It's curious but in my memory of that moment, those objects seemed to have had little flickering lights inside that made me think of the abdomen of the fireflies (lightning bugs?) that I captured in jars long ago on such summer nights as this. Ricky and I helped ourselves but Chuck abstained. He was a frequent-flyer but he would sit this one out.

Once the main festivities had concluded and the lightweights had gone home, we, the remaining stalwarts, sat on a blanket out in the grassy backyard near the lake. Tiny lake waves lapped at the railroad ties of the dock and breezes toyed with our hair. Upon this magic carpet sat band members, girlfriends, assorted hangers-on and complete strangers, each transfixed in childlike rapture by this starry night with its abundance of wonders. Ricky held court from the carpet's center. This was a guy who could pull off wearing a caftan in a New England mill town at the tail end of the Sixties—and with his long hair and thick beard he looked every inch the part of hippie guru.

Our magic carpet may have been anchored to the Earth by our physical forms, but the planet managed to spin its spinning self around the sun and thus across the whirling universe as the stars wheeled about over our heads, grouped as they were in their little Greek myths.

We clung to that carpet the same way we clung to our seats when the park's roller coaster cars would rattle and clack over to that first big drop. The Flyer Comet, brightly lit on the far side of the lake, was now making its way around to do just that—*too late to turn back now.* Its passengers would either feign nonchalance, scream or hold their arms up defiantly like victorious prizefighters. Their screams and the roar of the coaster cars were only faintly audible to us from where we sat across the water.

☙

Upon regaining consciousness, I found myself standing stock still like an actor on his mark waiting to deliver a line that he'd forgotten as the first flickers of dawn illuminated the sky to the color of aluminum. Although the sun hadn't broken the horizon yet, the sky reflected off of the lake's rippling surface and cast disco ball reflections dancing all over the yard, the back wall of the cottage and the three of us. Ricky was kneeling down on the beach, plunging his hands into the lake and scooping out palmfuls of water—awestruck by what he beheld. I became aware of a newfound ability to see each blade of grass individually. Breezes off the lake were cutting rivulets though them and capriciously parting them like you'd part hair with a blowdryer. Chuck was watching protectively over his brother and me and smiling in amusement at these wide-eyed pilgrims. The breeze was playing with one lock of hair on his forehead and he looked to me like one of those gold-leafed Russian Orthodox icons of Our Lord and Savior. It was now just the three of us because the rest of the revelers had scored rides and split—leaving the three stooges stranded at the lake.

With a phone call Ricky managed to reach his ex-wife whom he cajoled into starting her workday painfully early in order to give us lifts home. She drove a black Pontiac of a early-Fifties vintage that shone like new. Her former husband and she were only recently split and they both seemed to be self-consciously making an effort not to act like a married couple while learning the ropes of this their new relationship. It was kind of awkward to watch to be honest. I chatted with her a little until Ricky accused me, *in...a...very...calm...voice,* of hitting on her right in front of him which I, of course, denied. Ricky didn't buy it but said that it was all right—he just wanted me to know that he knew—that was all.

I may have drifted in and out of slumber a couple of times during this ride but the blackness that should have been on the insides of my eyelids was now replaced by colorful hissing video static through which Ricky's panicky face would occasionally plunge to reassure me with soothing pronouncements such as: *"WE OH-DEED ON THIS SHIT MAN!"* My guru was letting me down.

They dropped me off in front of the Fairmount Café where mostly out of necessity I'd briefly been crashing with a young woman that I scarcely knew in her apartment on the third floor. As the shining Pontiac from the past pulled away from the curb, I looked down the street at the row of storefronts before mounting the stairs. Huge paisley-covered apostrophe-shaped chrome balloons sprouted up from the bases of the buildings and then dwarfed them. The slumbering village of Cleghorn was having its own Macy's parade down Fairmount Street for its only audience and I felt almost guilty. Although the colors in the shapes were rather uninspiring grays and earth tones that may have been reflective of that wan barrio—I also instinctively knew that the color dulling might also signal the winding down of my own personal "Flyer Comet" ride.

⚓

She'd already left for work by the time I arrived and the only trace of her was a half-empty box of chocolate-covered doughnuts, which during our brief acquaintance, was the only thing that I'd ever seen her eat. It was already getting too hot and stuffy on the top floor so I went out onto the back porch to eat a doughnut and get some oxygen. There was a five-story brick factory building on the other side of this shallow, boulder-strewn stretch of the Nashua River. It was over half-a-mile away but with my newly acquired super-vision I could see the building's every brick and the mortar that bound them. If required to, I'm sure I could have counted them all.

An enormously corpulent woman appeared at one of the top story windows and perched there with her plump arms cradling her huge bosom. Even at this distance she spotted me immediately and started waving and calling to me excitedly—her voice echoing off the buildings and river bottom—the skin flab-a-dabbing on her arm. In my paranoia the last thing I wanted was any attention paid to me so I played possum and pretended not to notice her until she finally gave up, turned, and with a disgusted gesture with her hands, disappeared back into the building to do whatever it was that she was supposed to have been doing.

There were two apartments on the third floor of the

240

Fairmount building that shared the back porch and the screen door of the neighboring one squeaked open. Out popped a somber little girl of perhaps nine. She was dressed for church in a navy blue dress with white polka-dots, white shoes, socks and gloves, handbag and even white-framed dark sunglasses. Happily she totally ignored my presence and instead went over to the porch rail, struck a pose and stared intently at the factory building, perhaps looking for the fat lady. When her mother called she went back inside, squeak-slamming the screen door behind her. I also went inside and crumpled onto my cohabitant's couch exhausted.

❦

*Coda:*

*Later on that day, Mike, our guitarist, and Chuck showed up at the apartment minus Ricky who was also probably crumpled on some couch somewhere. I was strung out from the party and the guys were good-naturedly making fun of everything I said and being too weak to jab back I just sort of absorbed the ribbing.*

*We lived on music then and since there was a stereo in the living room we spun the only album this girl owned which happened to be the Beatles latest release,* Let It Be. *We blew off that sweltering afternoon back in the day laughing and playing those songs over and over—practicing the harmonies in that drab little parlor on Fairmount Street.*

*James Dean memorial*

# CHOLAME

*Prelude:*

  On September 30, 1955, James Byron Dean's meteoric rise to film stardom was cut short when his newly-acquired Porsche Spyder collided with a Ford outside of Paso Robles in Cholame, California. Jimmy's intended destination had been a sports car competition at Salinas where he planned to enter the car marked with a 130 and the nickname "Little Bastard." At first he planned to trailer it to the race but had opted for photographer Sanford Roth to shadow him north with the empty trailer in tow. He did not take the scenic route up the coast—he wanted to shake out his new toy on 466 where he could open it up a little.

  When the driver of a two-toned Ford, Donald Turnupseed, made the decision to make the left onto 41 from 466 he had misjudged the speed at which the Spyder was barreling at him. Dean had taken for granted that the Ford would give him the right-of-way until he passed before making its turn. Porsche mechanic Rolfe

*Wurtherich was riding shotgun that day. Wurtherich (who was thrown from the vehicle in the crash) survived and later recounted that the young actor had yelled "That guy up there's gotta stop; he'll see us," as the Ford began to lumber across the white lines. It was the actor's last spoken line on Earth. At 24 he had lived up to his credo to, "live fast, die young and leave a good-looking corpse." It was 5:45 p.m.*

🐝

**In the summer of 1990** I was given a two-week assignment to edit a technical manual at a company facility near Santa Barbara. The job entailed physically pasting type corrections into an existing mechanical board and was a real blast-from-the-past kind of project execution-wise. The tools were: an IBM Selectric (with a type ball), an X-acto knife and a can of rubber cement. It was the worst type of Kamikaze/Nazi-Frankenstein paste-up job and represented the last time that I would use a drawing board to do my work. The time would pass however and it was a chance to see a bit of California (to which I'd never been nor been back to since). The middle weekend was approaching and I kicked around ideas for keeping myself amused with the guys in the office offering suggestions.

Disneyland came up and although I had told my mother in no uncertain terms back in 1955 that I was definitely going there after seeing it being constructed on the *Mickey Mouse Club* program, I was finally getting my opportunity—and balking. It was a few decades late in coming I'm afraid. Anyway that's a place you bring kids to. They described the Hearst Castle which sounded interesting and would put me on the Pacific Coast Highway heading north which I liked the idea of. I brought up my interest in the James Dean accident site in what I remembered as being at Paso Robles but they knew to be Cholame. Bear in mind that this was pre-Google era.

🐝

On Saturday morning I took off with my sketchy plan that might (or might not) involve San Francisco as a final

244

*Cholame*

destination. Along the way I spotted some zebras in the fields off the road and knew I was either having an acid flashback or approaching the Hearst property at San Simeon. I pulled into the vast parking lot but upon seeing that tour busses would be a necessary component of the experience, made a U-turn and pulled back onto the PCH.

I had always assumed this would be the route that James Dean would have chosen on his way to the races at Salinas but this was not the case. Still, I was happy to have a solid destination on that beautiful day. At San Luis Obispo I turned towards Route 41 and Cholame and as I got closer my mind drifted back to 1961.

When James Dean died in 1955, I was all of eight-years-old and had more interest in *The Mickey Mouse Club* than him or the circumstances of his death. His was just another face in my mother's movie magazines. I did have one faint memory about the blond actor in a red jacket and cars driving off of a cliff, so maybe someone had taken me to see *Rebel Without a Cause*, but I'm sure the plot would have been over my head.

But something happened in 1961. Maybe I was at an age where I was feeling alienated, angry and seeking something with which to relate when I caught a TV broadcast of *Rebel* and a light went on in my head. It was like I was somehow seeing myself in the flickering pixels. I started seeking out his other movies—*Rebel's* bookends: *East of Eden* and *Giant*. Occasionally there were special showings of his work from back when he was cutting his teeth on live television but they were few, far between and therefore to be savored. I started assembling a scrapbook torn from old magazines. I was finding them in used book stores by grabbing handfuls of publications from 1955 and going through page-by-page in the event that there would be a snippet here or a picture there. My girlfriend's older sister donated her collection to mine and so it expanded. Geno and I even went on a special mission to find archived

245

articles at the Leominster Public Library. He ripped out a plum spread from *Life Magazine*, stuck it into his motorcycle jacket and we jumped out the back window. Such was the extent of the obsession.

I started to ape Jimmy's patented slouch, scrunched my face into contorted, tortured expressions and pulled my hair out by the roots trying to make it look like his. With my conk perfected, my facial muscles trained into a Deanish rictus and my voice altered to approximate his nasal Hoosier drawl, all that was needed was a cherry on the top—that Technicolor red windbreaker—and it wasn't hard to find.

Looking back on those days with the objectivity of time, it all must have seemed kind of...*eerie*. I can even remember a high school counselor expressing concern over this idolatry of a dead man to which I just shrugged my shoulders. You either got it or you didn't. My mother was actually disappointed to see me abandon my allegiance to Elvis, whom she'd come to like, but for me at that time, the singer seemed to have lost his relevance.

Over the years, I have come to learn that the James Dean that I had deified from his movies bore little resemblance to the star in real life. I came to see the confident, competitive, articulate actor, bursting with talent, moody, complex and wide open to life. His art was more than what he put up on the screen and stage; his greatest masterpiece would be himself, *man as Art*. Moreover he was far cry from the hurt/vengeful boy of *East of Eden*, the rebel/hero trying to be accepted in the painfully dated *Rebel Without a Cause* or the lovelorn rags-to-riches punk he portrayed in *Giant*. Dean is not without his detractors, but long after my obsession passed, he remains an acting genius in my estimation. If you can touch someone's life with your art to the degree that he had mine it's an achievement worth noting.

&

Now in Cholame I looked for landmarks along the highway. I knew that I was near the scene of the accident and I noticed a little diner on my left so I drove down to the next intersection to turn around. I didn't know it at the time but that's where the crash occurred. I went into the restaurant and sat at the counter figuring I'd get a hamburger and a beer and maybe make a little small talk about the famous actor who had died nearby. There was a small amount of memorabilia on the walls to look at while I waited but after a while when no one came to wait on me I got up and left. Outside in the yard of the diner there was a scrubby looking tree that had a large abstract chrome sculpture wrapped around it dedicated to Dean. A bronze plaque nearby explained that it was a gift from his fans in Japan. There were only a few people milling around and it occurred to me that this would be an appropriate moment for a symbolic gesture. I would leave my red windbreaker (one of a long line of many—this one with a polo player on the breast) on the sculpture as an offering and leave, thus marking the end of an era. I walked over and removed my jacket, hung it on the memorial, took a picture of it then turned my back and went to my car.

&

*Coda:*

*The physical death of James Dean marked the birth of his legend. He'd only lived to see one movie released which was* East of Eden, *perhaps his best. Because of his startling death at a young age, the debut of* Rebel Without a Cause *created a sensation. Today there are still remembrance rallies in Fairmount, Indiana where he was born, while in California devotees still make the (somewhat morbid) drive up 46 retracing Dean's stops along the way as if they were the Stations-of-the-Cross: Donut at the Farmer's Market; site of the speeding ticket; Blackwell's Corner for apples and Coca-Cola; haunted Polonio Pass and finally the crash site itself. But his fans are growing old now and dwindling in number. He has no oldies on the radio, no major tourist attractions, or (Heaven help us) James Dean impersonators to perpetuate his memory or generate new fans. There remain only a handful of films that may or may not have stood the test of time to define his legacy. Whatever one's judgment of them may be, I maintain that Jimmy's power and artistry in those roles still hold up.*

*It would be more poetic to say that that's where the story of my impromptu pilgrimage ends—but it isn't. Actually I sat in my rental for a while with the engine idling, looking over at the sculpture reflecting the California sun with my red jacket fluttering in the breeze from an appendage. It was no use. I got out of the car, retrieved the jacket and drove off in the direction Monterrey.*

*Although I haven't worn it since, the Technicolor red windbreaker hangs in my cellar to this day, a vestige of my youth, smelling old as do all the yellowing magazine clippings that I still keep in a cardboard box on a shelf. I can't seem to bring myself to throw them out...yet.*

*War is Hell*

# HULA HULA

*Prelude:*

*In the way of a child, I became acquainted with the objects housed between the somber large floral print papered walls of Nana's parlor in her little Mansard-roofed cottage at 34 Sprague Street in West Fitchburg. There was the formal photograph of her parents peering skeptically back at the camera posed back in Knockmanagh, Ireland (which Nana referred to as the "Auld Sod") from a heavy oval oak frame. In the place of honor over the couch hung a framed print of Our Lord Jesus sitting on a rock in the moonlight comforting a flock of sheep. I would not have understood the symbolism of that imagery, but he seemed very nice and gentle to the animals and they looked content. There were fronds from Palm Sunday twisted into cruciforms tacked to the walls or tucked behind pictures. A couple of mysterious gallstones graced her bookcase. And then there was the wizened coconut always near the foot of the radiator under the only window in the room. The coconut always so alluring in the way of a football that you couldn't help but touch. It was what you might call a satisfying object—withered as it was with age but preserved with varnish somewhere along the line. Closer observation revealed cryptic etchings on its sides. When I had asked Nana about them she informed me that this son had carved the year, 1944, the place Honolulu, Hawaii and his name, Raymond Gallagher, during an idle moment, long ago while serving in World War II. Ray had brought it back to the states once the war had ended as a souvenir.*

&

**My Uncle Ray was born** into a working-class family. My grandparents, Hugh and Hannah, had emigrated from Ireland and met and married in America. Grandpa found work at the Crocker Paper Company and stayed on through to his retirement. Their eighth-born grew to be a handsome devil who had no qualms about reminding anyone who would listen of that fact. By all accounts he had a great left hook which came in handy when things got out of hand down at the British-American Club or the Log Cabin when he and younger brother Edward would cover each other's backs during the drunken brawls that more often than not enlivened Saturday nights down along the river. This neighborhood of Irish immigrants, where to this day people are fond of the war cry, "West Fitchburg Against The World," did not suffer sissies.

After Pearl Harbor, patriotism ran hot in the United States and young men did not wait around to be drafted into service— and although Ray had to leave high school to do so—he and brother Edward enlisted in the Navy. Quiet Eddy drew service in the North Atlantic freezing his ass off escorting convoys while—ever the fair-haired son—Ray drew Hawaii. To the best of my knowledge he never saw combat and the family joke was that he spent the war doing the Hula-hula.

My mother had a great photograph of him that he'd sent home from Hawaii. In it he is sitting in the front seat of a jeep with two other guys in a palm-fringed airfield. They are shirtless and my uncle has a service-issue .45 Colt automatic dangling from his right hand in front of the windshield and smiling his movie star smile. The barroom boxing still served him well too for (by his account) he'd become fleet boxing champion in his weight class! To put things into perspective though: he was somewhat prone to what the Irish call *blarney*.

My uncle Ray exemplified this parable that little brother Bob quoted during his eloquent eulogy of his big brother. It's called an Irish Tribute and it's a good-natured Irish take on the *Book of Genesis* and the Irish place in the scheme of things. In the beginning it goes...

*...then God made man. The Italians for music and art; the French for fine food; the Germans for intelligence; the Swedes for their beauty; the Jews for their religion and so forth until he considered what he had created thus far and realized that no one was having any fun—and so he decided to make an Irishman.* Someone like Ray was probably what he had in mind.

He had an entrepreneurial spirit and chased his dreams to the West Coast in the early-Fifties—along with his wife and four children. On one jaunt he had run out of gas in the hinterlands outside of San Diego. His wife was not with him and he was going to have to go and find some fuel and bring it back in a Jerry can. The kids were understandably apprehensive about being left alone, but he reassured them that he would be right back and that to stay brave they should sing the plucky Irish novelty song "Who Put the Overalls in Mrs. Murphy's Chowder?" until he did. Ray then determinedly hiked off down the hot, dusty highway on his quest with the sound of his children's singing fading into the distance. Everything worked out fine though and this incident became the stuff of family lore.

֎

*Coda:*
*Many years later, Ray's children had gathered around him again; but this time by his hospice bed. My uncle's life was near its*

*end and his kids were with him as he lay on it breathing his last. As he was taken off life support, they were each talking to him, encouraging him on to that final destination, while son Randy began to sing "Mrs. Murphy's Chowder." Amazingly enough, he remembered every single lyric and he was able to sing the entire song before his father had taken his last breath. Thus, in the end, my Uncle Ray departed life with a song, much as he had lived it.*

*I should acknowledge that this story borrows liberally from my Uncle Bob's eulogy for his fallen sibling. That and his other remembrances of the Gallagher clan growing up have been eye-opening and inspiring.*

*Rink, me and Vic*

# POOR LITTLE FOOL

*Prelude:*

*With the amps and PA lugged, plugged and sound-checked, we had 30 minutes to kill before taking the stage at the O.K. Corral in Peabody, Massachusetts for its New Year's Eve party. Traditionally, nightclubs (read: barrooms) book their most popular bands for that night and in 1985, we were it: the Boston Rockabilly Music Conspiracy (B.R.M.C.). The band was the brainchild of Vic, the piano player/band leader, and his mission was to keep alive the music that first inspired him (and the rest of us): Rockabilly and early Rock and Roll. Rink (rhythm guitar); Chuck (drums) and I (bass) were the founding members with Jimmy now joining us on lead guitar.*

*I did a mean Elvis and Vic was an acolyte of "The Killer" himself: Jerry Lee Lewis, but around their songs our repertoire was made up of classics by the other greats of the time and genre; Eddie Cochran, Buddy Holly, Gene Vincent, Carl Perkins, Fats Domino,*

*Chuck Berry and even Ricky Nelson. I qualify with that word "even" because although I always liked Rick's records, it was like he had joined the party late and was somehow acting the part of Rock and Roll singer on his parent's TV show* The Adventures of Ozzie and Harriet. *As good as he was in his own right, he didn't seem to fit into the same category as his contemporary rockers.*

*Along with his mastery of the boogie-woogie piano, Vic played rhythm guitar as part of the show and in that casual moment before we went on he reached for his black Takamine and started strumming...C-A-minor-F-G; the simple progression to myriad pop songs, but when he started to sing along it was revealed to be Nelson's "Poor Little Fool" to this little audience comprised of the rest of B.R.M.C. Although "Hello Mary Lou" and "Travelin' Man" were on our setlist, the song he was singing wasn't—he'd just pulled it out of his hat. It sounded pretty sweet and we were chirping in some harmonies out of habit. After he'd finished we all climbed onto the stage to tune up, plug in and play.*

⅋

**The Adventures of Ozzie and Harriet** was one those bland Fifties TV shows that had begun life on radio and although I have some nostalgic affection for it, O&H made *Father Knows Best* look like *King Lear* by comparison. The plots were painfully trivial, the acting amateurish, the humor so lame that you wondered what the tired-sounding canned laughter found so amusing. Even the film itself looked like it had taken too many spins in the washer. Their "adventures" never seemed to take them very far from the shopworn sets that were their living room, kitchen, driveway (hoop on the garage) and once in a while the exotic locale of the malt shop.

"Little" Ricky Nelson was the brightest light on that low-wattage show. He was a cocky little shit and one of his sardonic retorts made you laugh along with the laugh track at least once an episode. Ricky's signature comeback line was, "I don't fool around, boy."

Like myself, Rick was a fan and student of Elvis and as legend

254

has it, he'd brought a date to see one of Presley's performances and this girl was, well, impressed. Piqued by a bit of jealousy perhaps, he bragged that he could do that if he wanted and he went to work to prove it. In April of 1957, as part of the plot of *Ozzie and Harriet* he jumped onstage with a band and launched into Fat's Domino's "I'm Walkin'." That song was an excellent choice. Best not go head-to-head with *The Sideburned One* with one of *His* own songs, but there was no mistaking the King's influence. The close-ups reveal some teenage acne on his handsome if strangely inert face, but when the adoring camera does a wider shot during the guitar solo, Rick does a few conservative *Elvisesque* moves and the girls in the audience begin to squeal. He's clearly enjoying himself, as are his mom and dad, snapping their fingers in the wings, smiling and swaying. Former bandleader Ozzie Nelson sees the future of his flagging show and it is his youngest son. Sparkling dollar signs boogie in his eyes. Ricky, the experienced actor, put his own mellow cool into the performance and it had worked—he had made the song his own and for little Ricky Nelson, the worm had turned. For kids of my generation his metamorphosis did not go unnoticed as we prepared for metamorphoses of our own. He had come of age right in front of our eyes.

Even at that age though I smelled some kind of unfair advantage due to his television fame when his "Teenager's Romance" and "Be Bop Baby" hit the charts. They were enjoyable if callow efforts that I came to enjoy, threat to "The King" though they may have been. In time his musical fame eclipsed that of his starring role on the show and he truly became a singer of note. As such he rounded up a crack band for himself including James Burton on lead guitar and even had the uncredited Jordanaires (Elvis' backup singers, allowed by royal dispensation) sing behind him. In 1958 "Poor Little Fool" became his first number one single and sold two-million copies. He was now doing concerts for throngs of screaming, adoring, underwear-tossing girls, including one at the same venue where a year earlier he had bragged to his date that he'd soon be doing just that. That year Ricky had 12 chart hits as compared to 11 by Elvis—but to be fair—Private Presley was playing army in peacetime Germany—arguably not the best of career moves.

I'd make a special effort to be home in time to see the last 10 minutes of *Ozzie and Harriet* when they would show Rick singing his latest song: very nice promotion indeed. The songs helped the show, the show helped the song, and everybody left the table happy—especially Oz. For a while there Ricky had the playing field pretty much to himself: Elvis was in the Army; Buddy Holly, the Big Bopper and Richie Valens had died; Little Richard had found religion and Chuck Berry was in the slammer for violation of the *Mann Act*. He went on to amass 30 top-40 hits, surpassed only by Elvis and Pat Boone, until in 1964 the *British Invasion* stormed ashore and washed the old-timers away. Rick's career stalled after that as he struggled to find a new niche for himself. With the Folk-rocking Stone Canyon Band he released "Garden Party" which famously tells the story of a Madison Square Garden concert where, although he was doing his oldies, the audience nearly booed him off the stage because they didn't like his new long-haired, hippie image. It was a hit but it always struck me as something of a novelty record. From then on he tried different career tacks, but eventually, for income as well as to feed his *jones* for an audience, he went on the road and in the summer of 1985 that long journey would bring him to Newburyport, Massachusetts.

&

B.R.M.C. was a natural choice to open Rick's concert. We were a known entity in Newburyport having been popular at the Grog—the town's hottest nightspot. In addition we played the same type of music. So when the concert promoters needed an opener they got in touch. The show was part of Newburyport's annual Yankee Homecoming Week and was to be held in the football stadium behind the high school. We kicked off the show at sunset with the sky darkening and the stage lights brightening as we rocked along. The setlist was the cream of our repertoire, and the occasion brought out the fire in us so we did the hottest show ever to our biggest audience ever—about 3,000 oldies fans who filled the bleachers and the playing field.

Vic went as far as to stand up from the white baby grand during his solo and knock over his piano bench during "Great Balls of Fire." What a Killer moment! The crowd was enthusiastic and after we'd finished our set and walked off, they actually gave us a standing ovation and had summoned us back for an encore—pretty unusual for an opening act. I noted the fact over the PA saying, "Well that's a surprise!"

After the intermission, I went down and sat on the grass with my wife and some friends to watch Rick's show and to video tape it. The headliner did not let us down. He had adopted a retro image at this stage, sweeping back his hair and wearing black pants and shirt, a skinny pink tie and old-style tweedy-looking sport coat. Backed by his well-polished band, his set reminded you of all the hits he had back in the day and this audience adored him for it.

Following his own standing ovation and fiery finish we were invited back to his trailer if we cared to meet him and of course we all did. They lined us up near the door single-file and there were gaggles of his fans to either side of us. Some women in the crowd asked us to get his autograph for them and held out record sleeves and pens. Being musicians we felt too cool for such fan idolatry and shook our heads. "Hey, we come see you at the Grog" someone protested with the crowd murmuring in accord, so I reluctantly took a few items and stood waiting, now feeling like a geek.

It turned out that he was a great guy just as you might imagine, friendly with a good sense of humor. After taking some pictures, critiquing the show and comparing notes on the musician's lot there was a pause signalling that it was autograph time. I held up a couple of albums and a pen and Rick commented knowingly, "You got stuck, huh?" I smiled wryly and nodded.

⚘

Near Christmas of that same year, B.R.M.C. would be offered another opportunity to open for Rick. It would be at a cellar club in Harvard Square called Jonathan Swift's on a snowy, freezing Saturday night. It's lost to time whether we got the gig because the agent knew our music would be a good fit or whether Rick himself had perhaps remembered the Rockabilly band back in New England and had asked for us.

We got set up early and waited for the star to show up but he never did. Eventually his manager called the club to say that the rickety DC-3 in which the band toured the country was snowed in up at the airport in Buffalo. Without Rick there would be no show and the club owner dismissed us without pay. That didn't seem fair because we could have entertained whoever *did* come through the door that night but what with the weather and the cancellation, he must have figured that the night was a wash and that there was no profit in having us play to five patrons, a bartender and a waitress. Disappointed we packed our gear, lugged it up the stairs and out into that frigid winter night.

⚘

A few weeks later it was New Year's Eve and we had just begun our first set at the O.K. Corral. It was always my habit to gauge the audience's reaction to our show and on this night I could sense a ripple of excitement spreading from table to table like wildfire. I didn't find out what it was until someone came up and told us that news had broken on the *CBS Evening News* that Rick's plane had crash-landed and caught fire while on tour near DeKalb, Texas. The singer and his band, trapped in the plane, had died in the blaze. The road had claimed another one. I made the sad announcement over the PA but the whole audience already knew by then. In his honor we played "Travelin' Man" and "Hello Mary Lou."

&

That old airplane, a dual-prop DC-3 manufactured in 1944, was a sturdy workhorse but it had seen better days. By coincidence it had once belonged to Jerry Lee Lewis in his heyday. JLL had customized it in accordance with his *nouveau-riche* country boy standards and it was outfitted like a flying Cadillac Coupe de Ville. By '85 however it had become plagued by mechanical problems, one of which was a malfunctioning gas-fueled heater which probably started the fire. It was NOT however—as had gone the rumor—that the band had caused it by freebasing onboard. The pilot and copilot had escaped the downed and burning plane by breaking out through the cockpit windows and had gone to its side to see if they could get the passengers out but to no avail. They grew concerned that the fuel tanks would blow and had retreated. I can't imagine the hellacious nightmare that cabin must have been.

&

*Coda:*

*When we took our first break we talked about the concert the previous summer, Jonathan Swift's...and then about the way Vic had done that impromptu reading of "Poor Little Fool." He'd never done that before and never did again. It was kind of weird.*

*My Harmony Sovereign*

# SUN RECORDS

**The first time I ever saw** the Sun Records label—that orange rooster on a yellow background crowing the dawn—it wasn't on an Elvis Presley record; it was on Jerry Lee Lewis' piano-pumping Boogie-Woogie masterpiece "Whole Lotta Shakin' Goin' On." This was in my friend David's room where he, as I, was beginning a collection of little 45 RPM vinyl records with big holes. We kept them in little latch-locking boxes that had their own little filing systems.

Rock and Roll was in its infancy then and that was the first time that I'd heard "The Killer." It seemed like once Elvis hit the airwaves, the floodgates just opened and we were swept along by the torrent of new talent. There were Jerry Lee, Eddie Cochran, The Everly Brothers, Little Richard, Chuck Berry, Gene Vincent, Fats Domino, Buddy Holly, Carl Perkins and a host of one-hit-wonders whose trajectories may have faltered but who became immortal through one treasured gift—the hit record. There were so many in fact that it was getting hard to keep up. Each new record seemed a revelation. Rock and Roll was an unexpected gift to my childhood.

I was already a rabid Elvis fan but became one on the basis of his RCA Victor hits "Heartbreak Hotel," "Don't Be Cruel," "Too Much," and my nominee for the first true Rock and Roll song: "Hound Dog," along with his TV appearances of course. The fact that he'd started at Sun Records in Memphis before the owner (and Elvis discoverer) Sam Phillips controversially sold his contract to the larger label for $35,000 in order to promote his other artists (Lewis, Perkins and Cash) as well as to make other investments—such as the founding of Holiday Inn—was unknown information to me back then.

Elvis was a star that I felt I owned and was in fact an expert on, therefore I was dismayed to hear his "You're A Heartbreaker" coming from a radio inside my friend Larry's grandmother's house just across the peeling white picket fence that separated her yard from ours. "Is that Elvis?" I'd asked Larry across the fence.

"Yeah, he made some records before 'Hound Dog,'" he said. I was dumbstruck, and I realized that my education was incomplete. Somehow I found out that the songs were recorded and released by Jerry Lee Lewis' label, Sun, but there was no way to access them because they were out-of-print. But then RCA began releasing them on four-song extended-play (EP) 45s with cardboard sleeves just like their big brother long-playing record albums. They had bought the song rights from Phillips and were mining their new star's popularity for all it was worth by re-releasing his backlog. Fifty-thousand Elvis fans (with money in their hands) couldn't be wrong after all.

֎

On Thursdays, which were my father's paydays, my mother would rendezvous with him for the household split. This transaction occurred at a little restaurant on the second floor of a brick building on Main Street in downtown Leominster called Monty's Garden. With its staircase entrance, dark wood paneling, cozy booths and checkered tablecloths, the atmosphere made you feel like you were in an episode of *The Untouchables*. Jukebox terminals were at all of the booths and my mother fed me change to pump into the slot. There was some Rock and Roll but not much at that time. We used to eat toasted turkey-club sandwiches and she would always let me have the delicious Maraschino cherries that had been marinating in her Manhattans.

While she went about her business downtown, I took my few bucks of spending money (and my cherry buzz) over to M.M. Sabatelli's appliance store. They had a record shop in the basement and it was funny but every time I descended the stairs they seemed to be playing "Mister Lee" by the Bobbets like it was my theme song. There were isolation booths where you could listen to an album or 45 that you might want to buy (or if you just felt like listening to for fun). You'd just grab one, go into the booth, open the package and give it a spin. If you liked it, you bought it. If not you just said that you weren't interested and it went back into the rack without question. I didn't need to test Elvis though. If he sang it, the song was an automatic inclusion into my little latched box of 45s. When I'd get home, I'd listen to them over and over, learning every lyric and inflection. Until I got a guitar (a Harmony Sovereign bought with *Green Stamps*) of my own, I spent a lot of time in my room lip-synching his songs into my mirror while strumming my tennis racket, practicing my moves, my lip curl and training my hair into a *pompadour*.

My mother was a soft touch in some ways and if I felt like bagging school on a given day, she wasn't hard to convince with a forced sniffle or a bellyache complaint. In fact, I don't think she minded the company on her long days spent doing housework and watching TV. And so—though my grades began to falter—I was becoming a self-taught *Elvisologist*, a discipline that has served me ever since.

*Sun Studio in Memphis, 2006*

# MEMPHIS

**In 2006 I got a call** from a friend named Kevin with whom I'd had a couple of Rockabilly bands. He and his wife Kerri had pulled up stakes in Maine and put them down in Water Valley, Mississippi. They had the kinds of jobs that didn't require a trip to an office and with real estate high in Maine (as in Maine people can't afford to live in Maine), they found a nice spread at a reasonable price in the South and made the break. As much as anything, Kevin liked the idea of being near the birthplace of Rock and Roll: the Mississippi Delta.

He had a proposition for me. His band had a gig at a bar called the Windy City Grille in the little whistle-stop of Como, Mississippi and he wanted me to play bass with them. Since I live in Gloucester, Massachusetts, it is obvious that what the bar would pay would put me in the red factoring in travel expenses—but he sweetened the pot. Jocelyn and I could stay at their guesthouse, have a little vacation, swim in the pool, play the gig and get to see the Memphis attractions of Graceland, Stax Records and more importantly to me—the shrine itself—Sun Records Studios. In addition to this, Kevin was working on a CD of original songs and was going to record two of them at Sun and he wanted me to play bass on the session as well.

Sun is presently a museum during the day, but at night it comes to life as a working recording studio that swings into action after the museum hours are over, and as an additional incentive, Kevin was offering me an hour of studio time for a song of my choice.

It had been the hottest weather that I'd ever known back in Gloucester that summer and when we arrived in Memphis it was that much hotter. Having worked in Saudi Arabia I know hot. Kevin and Kerri picked us up at the airport and taxied us to their home. Between seeing Graceland, touring Stax, playing the gig in Como and eating ribs on Beale Street and catfish at the Taylor Grocery, we cooled ourselves by their pool and ran though what we were going to do in the studio. We rehearsed in the guesthouse now joined by his drummer, Eddie.

୶

We were about as ready as we were going to be. The daytime crowds were gone and it was just the three of us there to lay down basic tracks for two of his songs for the CD. More tracks were to be layered on at a later date. Our engineer, James Lott, exchanged pleasantries as he shuffled microphones and amplifiers around the room. The walls and ceiling are covered with old-style soundproofing with the ceiling having several "scallops" that reminded me of a Conestoga wagon—old-school sound design.

The engineer's booth was elevated about six steps where a large window had a commanding view of the studio floor. Marion Keisker's reception office, complete with retro details, is still out in front. That's where young Elvis made his first inquiries about making a record for his mother's birthday—as goes the legend. This studio was a room I'd been catching glimpses of all my life and is the most familiar place to which I'd never been. It's also one of those spaces that's been spared by neglect. Despite its musical significance, after its glory years the space was used to store tires, among other mundane uses. Now it is largely the same as it had been back in the day except for the big black and white photos of the artists who recorded there framed on the wall where they can kind of keep an eye on things.

Some call "Rocket 88" the first Rock and Roll record and it was recorded at Sun. Elvis, Johnny Cash, Carl Perkins, Jerry Lee Lewis and Roy Orbison laid down their tracks on its linoleum floor. U2 recorded "Angel of Harlem" in this hallowed hall and John Mellencamp put down several songs from his 2010 album *No Better Than This* here, going as far as using old-fashioned analog recording equipment for authenticity. The place is a Mecca to a lot of musicians.

We spent the hours it took to record the bass, rhythm guitar, drums and vocal tracks in a sweltering night that refused to cool off. With the main order of business attended to, we turned to my song. It would have been appropriate for me to have sung a Presley tune from his Sun sessions, but we were somewhat limited by our instrumentation so I decided on one by Chuck Willis instead called "What Am I Living For?" It seemed a little more within the grasp of our stripped-down combo. If it came out good enough I could always go back and add more instruments to the mix I figured (although I never did). Kevin and Eddie went up into the control booth to buzz about the recordings with James while I remained on the studio floor waiting to track my vocal. The lights were turned off so that the only illumination came from the big rectangular window where Sam Phillips once played puppeteer to his sideburned *protégés*. With my Sun idols looking down on me from the walls, ghostly in the dim light, James intoned: "Annnnnd...rolling."

On a four-count the instruments flowed in through my

headphones and after a measure I started singing. I wasn't on Elvis' actual microphone, *but*, I *was* standing in the same place where he'd once recorded "That's All Right Mama" and scores more. Crossed strips of black tape now mark that famous spot.

It was midnight in Memphis and it must have still been close to 90 degrees. I sweated through one take. Once the instruments stopped ringing James chimed in through the "cans" asking me if I wanted to take it again, but it seemed to me to be about as good as I could sing it so I just climbed the stairs for a listen over the big control booth speakers.

I closed my eyes and concentrated on the playback along with James at the soundboard. When it ended I asked for his opinion of the recording. He made an expansive gesture toward the big photos of the great artists of Sun on the walls and said, "You sound like them." I took that as high praise indeed.

*Irene Gallagher*

# GOOD NIGHT IRENE

**When I became old enough** to walk, Helen and Tony had a dazzling white picket fence built around the house to keep their little "Platinum Prince" from wandering off. Once I had a photograph showing me perched on the knee of one of the carpenters as he posed proudly with his new construction. As I collected my pictures for this book, it struck me that the fence was a recurring *leitmotif*—always standing protectively in the background, fading and peeling over time as we both grew older. By the time I left home, it had become ramshackle enough for me to kick down what had not already fallen on its own.

In the pictures taken inside the house there are repeat appearances of droopy, tinsel-draped Christmas trees loitering in the backgrounds. We always had one and a treasure trove usually awaited me beneath its boughs on Christmas mornings. The only exception being the year that my stepfather hit a slump at the track and there wasn't enough money to buy anything. That year they just pretended that the holiday didn't exist at all and skipped the whole affair—gambling that I wouldn't notice. It was actually possible in those days before the Christmas hype machine started churning out the advertising just after Halloween as it does today. If you were a preschooler in the early-1950s you could easily have missed it, and that year I did. Besides, there were only two channels on our big box television console with its little round screen, and half the time they were broadcasting an Indian-head test pattern.

Neither my stepfather nor my mother carried a driver's license so we didn't have a car. In my Dad's case it was because of an accident of birth that left him without the use of his right arm, greatly complicating driving the cars of that era which commonly had standard transmissions. Tony worked as an executive in the plastics company that he and his brother Dom inherited from their father: the Victory Button. One reason for buying the house on French Hill was because it was within walking distance to the plant, which had been relocated from Seventh to nearby Carter Street and re-christened Tamor Plastics. Rather than taking the long way and connecting with Carter from Sixth, you could access it by walking to the end of Seventh and clambering down a steep, rough embankment where the road ended. Anthony would take this dusty shortcut dressed in one of his dozen or so suits, expensive wing tips and—as would befit a man of his position—a *fedora*.

Despite Tony's handicap, if a hand was extended to him as a greeting, he had a charming way of shaking it with his left and smiling radiantly, transforming a potentially awkward moment into a wondrous one. My mother told me that she was amazed by the fact that on trips that they'd made to New York and Chicago, he would always run into people he knew on their sidewalks. Somehow people knew this son of the Plastic City wherever he went. Legend had it that he was acquainted with the gangster "Lucky" Luciano whose name I knew from watching *The Untouchables* on TV. There may have been some Italian stereotyping going on in that but I never heard him deny the assertion.

In our house entertainers were revered. My mother was always singing around the house just as she had when she and her siblings had cleaned up the kitchen after dinner in the big company-owned house on Baltic Lane in West Fitchburg where they grew up. That might have been one of the reasons that he loved her so much. My father did an uncanny impersonation of Louis Armstrong and when he'd sing "I'm Confessin' That I Love You" around the house, his face would absolutely transform into Satchmo's. Throw Elvis into the mix and man we were all singing!

⅋

When Helen was a young woman, she and her sisters—Irene and Peggy—went searching for adventure in Chicago. It was a three-contestant beauty contest amongst them but the consensus seemed to have been that Irene took first place. They hit some hard times out there though and my mother told me that when they were starving with little money, they would go into a diner and order cups of hot water and nickel cigarettes. Pouring catsup from the table into the hot water, they mixed their own tomato soup, smoked their butts and stayed out of the bone-numbing "Hawk" for a spell.

They had husbands by then, one of whom was my biological father—let's just call him "The Outlaw."My mother endured the stress of him sleeping with a .38 under his pillow or summoning his cohorts to the apartment to plot potential heists. Cinematic as this all must have seemed at the time—and no doubt exciting—the guns, ropes and masks they had stashed in a box in a closet were no movie props.

After the thrill of the new wore off, the impoverished way in which they were living and the stress of conditions in general began to take their toll on them physically and emotionally. Both Irene and her bartender husband contracted Tuberculosis from which neither recovered. Here there is history that I can't detail or only know in bits and pieces, so rather than fill in the dots for the sake of this story, will say instead that my mother's family prized discretion and that I will honor that tradition now. Leave it to be said that it was clearly time to call home.

My grandfather came out to claim the body of this, the beauty of his handsome brood, but he assigned the somber duty of escorting the casket home on a train to my young Aunt Peggy. Peggy and her father had their run-ins when she was growing up, but in spite of the fact that they'd bumped heads, Grandpa respected the way she had the pluck to stand up to him and so it was she that he entrusted with this grim responsibility. Tony, who had been a longtime suitor of my mother, then came swooping in to whisk delicate Helen home with kid gloves.

And with that the three sisters had returned home to Fitchburg: Irene to be laid to rest and my mother to eventually remarry—this time to the *Man* from Plastic City who always cared so well for her and in time for us both.

Only spunky Peggy went back to Chicago to establish a family where she lives to this day—still active in her nineties—an advocate for battered women and hospital volunteer, who reports that the sight of the Wrigley skyscraper lighting up the night sky still takes her breath away.

*Jocelyn and I, Madrid, 1988*

# MY PICTURES

**The images that I use** in *The Boy from Plastic City* are culled from my own collection—or what is left of it. You see; these come from my "uncool" album, the ones that didn't make the cut to the "cool" album. Around 1970 my old friend Geno, whose name you will recognize from some of the essays, borrowed my primary album for a while just to show someone the old shots.

During those times he was a member a biker club called the Slaves and there was a bloody turf war going on involving them and a rival club called the Nomads. Among the casualties of those hostilities was a van that Geno had been using to move some of his belongings from one apartment to another. One night the Nomads doused it with gas and torched it. Among the things destroyed in the blaze happened to be my album.

Geno handed me its unsalvageable remains as verification of its destruction. It was now just a waterlogged, misshapen gob of paper and melted plastic still dripping water and stinking of smoke which I plopped unceremoniously into a trash can. Even after losing most of his possessions, I could see that he felt worse about the fate of my album.

So what is left of my collection is an assortment of the rejects and old family photos and pictures garnered from my friends and family over the years. I feel that, cool or uncool, they tell a story of their own.

The picture that accompanies my story *"Omerta"* is from **Ray Johnson**. The gang picture on the front cover is from **Denis Dargis**. The back cover photo of me (in the goofy hat) is by **Dan Plumpton**.

Made in the USA
San Bernardino, CA
27 April 2016